"I like *The Leadersh*
larities between lea
in the business world. This isn't done very often, but it should
be. Another highlight of this book is the self-coaching questions,
which demand an internal response from the reader. This is an in-
depth, thought-provoking process. This book is sure to be used
by many current and future leaders."

—**James Sheets, President, JIMCO**

"*The Leadership Forge: Fifty Fire-Tested Insights* is a rare book. In
it, Joe Scherrer masterfully weaves fifty leadership insights he
gained during a sterling military career into a tapestry that speaks
clearly to leaders in all walks of life. The four-step model he uses
for each insight packages these words of wisdom into a format
that ensures both understanding and retention. He provides
a common ground on which leaders at all levels can meet one
another in the pursuit of meaning and truth. If you are already a
leader at any level, training to be, or aspire to be one, this timely
book is a must-read."

—**Michael Burroughs, Author,** *Before Onboarding: How to Integrate
New Leaders for Quick and Sustained Results;* **President, Burroughs
International; and Managing Director, Sheer Velocity Consulting**

"There are many books written about leadership, but none that I
have read translate the real-life experiences of an Air Force wing
commander into tenets that business executives and managers
can relate to on a daily basis. I was amazed at how well *The
Leadership Forge* captures, in a very refreshing and engaging way,
the wide variety of issues leaders confront in their careers. The
inspiring use of stories to frame each insight puts a perspective
on the insight that makes it real and removes it from the abstract.

This book is well written and will become your standard reference on the occasions when you encounter your own 'leadership crucible' events. You will find it a hard book to put down."

"Joe's many years of military service, including several assignments as a commander, allow him to blend vivid real-world lessons with his academic and historical knowledge. The result? A concise and comprehensive manual on leadership that is widely applicable to leaders of all kinds. Each chapter is a quick read, unpacking its concepts briefly and clearly so that the reader can rapidly grasp its key insights. In short, this is a helpful and thought-provoking guide on what it takes to be an effective, principle-centered leader."

"*The Leadership Forge* is packed with practical and inspiring leadership advice from a leader who's lived it. Punctuated with personal stories and packaged into easily applicable bites, *The Leadership Forge* will make you the leader you aspire to be!"

"I have absolute respect for Joe Scherrer's integrity, wisdom, and experience as a leader and commander. In *The Leadership Forge* he does a masterful job combining his own insights with wonderful stories, metaphors, and a great collection of suspenseful situations that bring leadership principles alive. Unlike so many leadership books, *The Leadership Forge* offers unique insights about leadership and serves them up in a practical way, offering a valuable guidepost for performance improvement and results—not to mention the fact that Joe's writing is inspiring and fun to read. This is a refreshing book that is hard to put down, and I can't recommend it enough."

—Andrew Neitlich, Founder and Director, Center for Executive Coaching

"Joe brilliantly synthesizes lessons from his Air Force career so leaders can apply them to their own challenges. In my experience working with hundreds of tech entrepreneurs, I have seen a strong correlation between those who embody the qualities described in *The Leadership Forge* and the fast acceleration of their ventures. Whether you are starting a new business or taking on greater challenges in a larger organization or in your personal life, this book provides key insights that can make the difference between success and failure."

—Jim Brasunas, Executive Director, IT Entrepreneur Network

"*The Leadership Forge: 50 Fire-Tested Insights* provides clear and compelling leadership insights that are applicable across all walks of life. Joe Scherrer provides a personal lens to leadership and enables readers to apply these insights through self-reflection. This is a valuable resource for all leaders who are committed to improving their skills and for new leaders who are on the skills development journey. Lastly, Joe's emphasis on each leader developing a personal leadership philosophy is particularly insightful: leaders should consciously deduce their own courses based upon their personal values and beliefs."

—Erik Stavrand, Stavrand Consulting

"'Mission First, People Always!' was a saying I had as a combat commander. This book provides thought-provoking insight on those words. Being a leader takes every ounce of effort for you to understand yourself, your people, and your situation. Joe's book gives the ingredients to allow you to grasp what it will take to see your full potential as a leader. No matter if you have been in a leadership position or are just beginning, you can't help but benefit from the insights."

—**James Appleyard, Director,**
Sales and Business Development, L-3 Communications

"We all know when we see great leadership. Great leadership produces high-performance organizations, and they're just not as common as we would like them to be. How do we produce more great leaders that we need so desperately right now? Joe Scherrer's book starts that process. Great leaders possess skills, traits, and competencies that make people trust them. This trust enables them to influence others. Leadership is a mindset, a way of living every minute of every day. It can be possessed by people in formal positions of authority as well as those at all levels of our organizations and communities. You don't need a title to lead effectively. Joe gives us ways to develop the skills and competencies of leadership whether you are the most junior member of the group or a more senior member who just hasn't thought about creating a personal framework."

—**Roger Ducey, Associate Professor,**
National Security Affairs, Naval War College

"*The Leadership Forge* is the kind of book you keep on your desk for a long time and revisit as situations arise. Filled with practical solutions based on real-world leadership challenges, Joe not only offers up theory based on research. He also gives clear action items for implementation. I've read my share of leadership books, and this is a rare find."

—Josh Turner, President, LinkedSelling

"Joe has done an outstanding job of whittling down key leadership principles to their essence and providing assessment guidelines that will help you as a leader learn and implement these principles critical to individual and organizational success."

—Jim Schneider, Former Junior National Team Cycling Coach and Owner, Pedal Hard

"In *The Leadership Forge*, Joe Scherrer explains how strong leaders master more than just their area of expertise; good leaders master the art of leading. Whether it's leading airmen as a commander in the US Air Force, leading students as a university lecturer, or leading executives as a business coach, with this book Scherrer shows once again that he's mastered the art of leading—and so will you."

—Kathy Ver Ecke, Owner, WorkingforWonka.com

"*The Leadership Forge* is a must-read for both up-and-coming leaders and those who have served in a leadership role most of their lives. Joe's leadership insights are applicable, motivating, and inspiring. Each leadership example and follow-up, self-coaching questions offer clarity and substance that develop leadership skills, heighten awareness, and demonstrate the power of successful leadership. *The Leadership Forge* offered a new perception of leadership for me that I will use in supporting others' leadership journeys."

—Belinda Gates, ACC Executive Coach and Author, *Your Successful Life: The Playbook for Defining and Achieving What Success Means to You*

"Joe Scherrer is a walking example of what it truly means to be 'an officer and a gentleman.' After a distinguished career serving in the United States Air Force, he now serves up a leadership book that's both thought-provoking and entertaining. Delving into scientific research as well as his personal experience, Scherrer provides a manual for all leaders, and potential leaders, to follow. *The Leadership Forge* is a great book to read, study, internalize, and reference often. Its self-coaching questions help you understand your journey, and Joe leads you down the right path."

—Ken Ohlemeyer, Account Director, Brighton Agency

"I've had the privilege of both working with Joe and enlisting his guidance as a professional coach. As I prepared for my current position, I put insights #13–16 into my leadership strategy, knowing my success is equally dependent on the performance of my enterprise partners as it is our own organization. Today I enjoy productive peer relationships and I'm operating effectively at one to two levels above my own."

—Tim Dickenson, Director, B-52 System Program Office

"Joe Scherrer is already known as an excellent executive coach and creator of leaders. Relying upon the same spirit of excellence that established his success as a highly decorated Air Force colonel, Mr. Scherrer leads by example throughout his first book. This is a leadership text that comes from the heart of a man who has experienced defeat and victory and has successfully led through each. *The Leadership Forge* offers a comprehensive set of 'fire-tested' insights to reproduce successful leadership practices in even the most inexperienced leader. For the seasoned veteran, it provides extremely practical guidance on how to apply valuable leadership lessons in everyday challenges. As an eager student and a harsh critic of leadership fads, I highly recommend *The Leadership Forge* as solid, time-tested guidance for all those who seek to serve their teams with integrity, courage, perseverance, and enthusiasm."

—Brett Barron, CEO, NGAGE

"Joe Scherrer has blended deep personal experience with carefully selected leadership ideas to produce a highly readable, punchy, 50-point guide to developing yourself as a leader. It's well written, lively, succinct, and thought-provoking."

—James Scouller, Author, *The Three Levels of Leadership: How to Develop Your Leadership Presence, Knowhow, and Skill,* and Principal, The Scouller Partnership

"Joe Scherrer had a very successful Air Force career not only by 'talking the talk,' but also by 'walking the walk' when it came to linking values and execution with his leadership performance. That comes out in this most readable, practical book, which I recommend for aspiring leaders and seasoned veterans."

—The Honorable Dr. Dale Meyerrose, Principal, The Meyerrose Group and Former Chief Information Officer to the Director of National Intelligence

THE
LEADERSHIP
FORGE

**50 FIRE-TESTED
INSIGHTS**

to solve your toughest problems,
care for your people, and get great results

THE
LEADERSHIP
FORGE

50 FIRE-TESTED INSIGHTS

to solve your toughest problems,
care for your people, and get great results

JOE SCHERRER

THE
LEADERSHIP
CRUCIBLE
PRESS

THE LEADERSHIP FORGE
50 FIRE-TESTED INSIGHTS to solve your toughest problems, care for your people, and get great results

ISBN: 978-0-9904896-1-0
Editor: Bobbi Linkemer, www.WriteANonfictionBook.com
Book design: Peggy Nehmen, n-kcreative.com

Published and distributed by:

THE LEADERSHIP CRUCIBLE PRESS

Saint Louis, Missouri
www.theleadershipcrucible.com

TO THE HOLY SPIRIT:
"ZELO ZELATUS SUM PRO DOMINO DEO EXERCITUUM"

TO DINA:
EU TE AMO

CONTENTS

PREFACE

A KNOCKING SOUND woke me from a deep sleep.

It was three o'clock in the morning on Christmas Day. Who would be calling at this hour? Some part of my brain told me it was a dream, so I laid my head down to go back to sleep.

But the knocking only got louder and more urgent.

I got up and went to the door to find my second in charge, Colonel Rick Folks, with a grim look on his face. I thought to myself, "Nothing good happens after midnight." And this wouldn't be good. Rick told me that one of the airmen on my staff had just committed suicide. I went numb. I said, "It's Christmas. Are you sure?"—hoping that it wasn't true. But it was.

At that point, all of my instincts as a military officer and commander of the US Air Force's only rapidly deployable communications wing kicked in. My questions came out in rapid fire, but inside, my heart was crushed because of the loss of one of my people and for the devastating impact this would have on his family. At the same time, as the leader of the wing, I knew that we needed to take decisive steps to deal with the aftermath of this tragic event.

This Christmas was going to be a tough one. But my challenges had only just begun.

The next day, I went into the office and pulled up my classified e-mail. There was a message that mentioned my wing. When I opened it, I discovered that headquarters had slated my unit of 1,500 highly trained airmen for closure.

As I had on Christmas Day, I reacted with disbelief. This couldn't be true. We had a global mission that was vital to the Air Force's ability to fly, fight, and win. But again, the news was accurate. Budget cuts and sequestration had driven some hard choices, and our mission had come out on the losing end.

For the rest of the week, I was barely able to sleep as I tried to wrap my head around all that had happened and still be the leader I needed to be. What made it especially tough was that I loved what I did—the mission, the organization, and especially my people—so receiving two heavy blows was hard to take. I found it impossible to separate the reality of what had happened from the emotional ties I had invested in the unit and its people.

In finding my way forward, I fell back on my faith and my values. In the Air Force, I had been taught to ground my ethos as an airman and as a leader on three core values: integrity first, service before self, and excellence in all we do. Those values, which found further meaning and depth in the context of my religious faith, were what I returned to as my touchstone in dealing with these difficult circumstances.

I also relied on some of the best friends and advisers that a commander could ever have: my vice commander, Colonel Rick Folks, and my Command Chief Master Sergeant, Quinton "Q" Otto, who was the senior enlisted airman in the wing.

Immediately, I made a commitment to handle the death and the closure with honor, dignity, and professionalism, in keeping with the respect deserved by those who serve and have served our nation.

LEADERSHIP IS A CRUCIBLE

That week was a real crucible—a difficult test—of my leadership. In a very real sense, so was my entire twenty-four-year Air Force career, as it is for everyone who has served in our armed forces, particularly those who have served in combat zones.

What I have come to realize is that whenever you assume the mantle of leadership, you will be placed in your own leadership crucible to be shaped, molded, and refined by the force of external and internal stresses. As part of this forging process, you will be tested over and over again in many different ways.

Much of what you experience will require struggle, effort, growth—and yes, even suffering. If you use the wisdom you gain from your ordeals well, you will not only emerge intact but also as a better, more capable, and more insightful leader.

Leadership—real, heroic leadership—is a tough business. But it is also a very gratifying business to know that as you make your way along your leadership journey, you are making your mark, moving the organization forward, and helping your people become better than they were the day before.

INTRODUCTION

THIS BOOK'S SUBTITLE states exactly what the book is about: to help you solve your toughest problems, take care of your people, and get great results. You will benefit from the fifty insights in this book by incorporating them into your personal leadership practice and growing as a leader.

This book is the product of my nearly three decades as an Air Force officer; multiple overseas deployments; and five assignments as a commander, including as a wing commander (a wing being the Air Force's primary war-fighting formation). It is also informed by the large body of academic research on leadership.

Each insight is structured as a self-contained lesson. You can read the book from start to finish, or you can select the insights that are most relevant to you or your situation.

Each insight is structured as follows:

- A leadership story pertinent to the topic
- A deeper explanation of the topic, to include relevant research
- A brief recap

- A few self-coaching questions to help you assess your understanding of the material
- A chapter-by-chapter list of recommended reading (at the back of the book) if you want to pursue a particular topic

This book's goal is to help you become the best leader you can be so you can mobilize people to achieve worthy goals.

If you are a leader, or aspiring to become one, this book is for you.

On to the insights!

INSIGHT #1

Leadership Is a Hero's Journey
Start Yours Now

"The big question is whether you are going to be able to say
a hearty yes to your adventure."
—Joseph Campbell

TAKE THE TIME to read or listen to some of the stories of our
nation's Medal of Honor winners, and you will find similar themes
running throughout all of them:

"What I did was nothing special."

"I did what anyone else would have done for me."

"There was no way I was going to leave anyone behind."

And perhaps most telling of all: "I'm not a hero."

But the fact of the matter is that they are heroes.

They demonstrated great courage in the face of fierce enemy
resistance. They disregarded their own welfare. They all acted not
for themselves but for those who needed help in life-threatening,
desperate situations. They demonstrated skill, courage, and
humility in the course of serving others while under tremendous
duress.

For many, to paraphrase the words of Lincoln, they gave "the last full measure of devotion." To be sure, our Medal of Honor winners provide us with a high standard for what it means to be a hero.

However, I argue that the best leaders are also heroes by virtue of the role they accept, the journey they take, and the trials that come with the territory. The best leaders are not in the business for personal glory or iron-fisted control. Rather, they lead because they seek to serve a higher purpose and use their unique gifts, talents, and skills to make a positive impact on their organizations and the people they encounter.

The leader as hero takes on a role that challenges competency, skill, and psychological mettle on a daily basis. Every day, in many large and small ways, the leader must face forces that endanger the success of the organization and the team. In this ongoing adventure, the leader-hero gives the gifts of credibility, vision, motivation, innovation, empowerment, and encouragement to the team.

In his book *The Hero with a Thousand Faces*, Joseph Campbell (1949) summarizes the hero's journey: "A hero ventures forth from the world of common day into a region of supernatural wonder; fabulous forces are there encountered and a decisive victory is won; the hero comes back from this mysterious adventure with the power to bestow boons on his fellow man."

Herein lies the leader's true power: giving of self to others.

DEEPER INSIGHT

First and foremost, leaders are required to take on responsibilities greater than themselves. Leadership is not easy, and in fact, it can be uncomfortable, even arduous. Leaders face tasks, trials, and challenges that are often intense, onerous, and unpredictable. Leaders face the stress of having to deliver results. Leaders must support the growth and well-being of the people they lead and deal with all of the drama and problems that inevitably arise. They do all of this with integrity, courage, and perseverance.

The journey can take place on a battlefield or in a maze of cubicles. It is lived out in myriad ways for myriad purposes. No two leaders have the same journey, but all leaders travel under the common bond of leadership.

In fact, it is in the performance of these daily leadership acts and in the perseverance required to accomplish them, despite the challenges to self and mission, that true heroism is displayed.

Although leaders such as Lincoln, Churchill, and King were tested in seemingly superhuman ways on the historical stage, I hold that the thousands of small acts of leaders like you are no less heroic.

Failure is as much a part of the leadership journey as success, and failure may be the most instructive part of it.

Perhaps most important, the leadership journey results in growth and change that yields maturity of purpose, deepening of wisdom, increased skill and competency, and humble awareness of limitations and dependency on others.

★ ★ ★

Leaders like you play out your vital role on the historical stage through your daily lives. Are you ready to commit to the journey?

RECAP

1. Leadership is a hero's journey.
2. Leaders are tested in ways that others are not.
3. The leader as hero is inherently selfless.
4. Being a leader means you take on responsibilities greater than yourself.
5. Heroic leadership takes place in the thousands of daily leadership acts that demand perseverance and courage despite challenges to self and the challenge of the situation.

6. Heroic leadership results in growth in wisdom, skill, and maturity driven by the difficulty of the journey itself.

SELF-COACHING QUESTIONS

1. Where are you on your leadership journey—just starting, well on your way, or at the end?

2. How does where you are on your journey influence the way you lead?

3. How deep is your commitment to leadership and all that comes with it?

4. What leadership challenges are you experiencing now that are demanding more from you in the way of selfless service, integrity, perseverance, and courage?

5. What are you learning from these challenges?

6. What can you do today to improve your ability to lead heroically?

INSIGHT #2

Get Clear on Your Leadership Sight Picture
*How to Power Your Leadership by Knowing Who You Are
and What You Stand For*

"At the center of your being you have the answer;
you know who you are and you know what you want."
—*Lao Tzu*

AFTER I WAS in the Air Force a while, I kept hearing a lot of the senior officers in meetings ask, "What's the sight picture on this?" or "What's your sight picture?" At first, I had no idea what they were talking about, but I soon figured out that, for a pilot, a "sight picture" is the relationship of the nose of the aircraft to the horizon; or in the case of a fighter jet, it's the relationship of the jet to an opposing jet or a bombing target.

A good sight picture is essential to ensure that the aircraft is heading in the right direction, at the right speed, and at the right altitude to reach or hit the target. It takes all of a pilot's training and senses to maintain a proper sight picture. A pilot that keeps it true will arrive at the destination or hit the target. A pilot that lets it drift will be off course and in potential danger.

Once I understood this, I adopted the sight picture metaphor as part of my leadership approach. Having a clear sight picture of who I was and what I stood for kept me oriented to my fundamental purpose as a leader and headed toward my goals. Surprisingly, most leaders take little or no time to understand themselves and thereby miss the opportunity to take their leadership to higher levels of competence and maturity.

The process of achieving your leadership sight picture deepens your self-awareness. As each component of your picture is assembled, you build a comprehensive understanding of how and why you operate. As you uncover new layers of personal insight, you set the stage for true self-mastery. The result of this process is a transforming view of your identity that can take your leadership to whole new levels.

Getting clear on your sight picture is really where it all begins if you want to improve as a leader.

DEEPER INSIGHT
Here is an overview of what I call the leadership sight picture.

- **Innate personality:** Few would argue that your personality is critical to your ability to lead. Personality is innate; it is also the aggregate of all the decisions you have made, your experiences, what you felt about those decisions and experiences at the time, and how you remember them. Personality remains fairly consistent throughout life, which means there is recognizable regularity to your personality. From a self-awareness perspective, it is vital that you gain at least some insight into your personality because it fundamentally affects how you present yourself to the world. It is also greatly influences how others see and respond to you.

- **Motivators:** We're all familiar with the basic human needs for food, water, and shelter. But professional success as a leader requires that your most important psychological needs are also met on a regular basis. From that perspective, understanding your underlying motivations is key to matching your needs to your actions and goals. It stands to reason that if your psychological needs are met, you'll be able to tap into your internal resources more readily, better focus on your responsibilities, and enjoy your work more.

- **Cognitive intelligence:** Academic research has shown that cognitive intelligence is one of the factors that correlate to leadership. Cognitive intelligence is an important leadership characteristic, particularly when it comes to unpacking and solving complex problems. Intelligence is also one of the best predictors of general job performance (Schmidt & Hunter, 1998). Being smart doesn't mean that you have to be a genius, but it does mean that it's to your advantage to be smarter than the average bear.

- **Emotional intelligence (EQ):** Intelligence quotient (IQ) is a measure of an individual's intellectual, analytical, logical, and rational abilities. EQ is the aspect of ourselves that enables us to make our way successfully in the world in terms of our relationships with others. In everyday language, emotional intelligence is referred to as "street smarts" or "common sense" (Stein & Book, 2011). Research studies have demonstrated that EQ predicts effective transformational leadership skills (Barling, Slater & Kelloway, 2000) and that its absence is related to career derailment (Ruderman, Hannum, Leslie & Steed, 2001). Knowing your EQ can be very useful to a leader.

- **Strengths:** A strength is a capacity for feeling, thinking, and behaving in a way that allows optimal functioning in the pursuit of valued outcomes (Snyder & Lopez, 2010). Dr. Martin Seligman, the founder of positive psychology, holds that your strengths are central to having good character and experiencing well-being. By identifying your strengths, you will be able to put them in play, be at your best most of the time, and add to your value as a leader.

- **Blind spots:** Blind spots are those aspects, usually negative, of your personality or your behavior that are known to others but not to you. Said another way, blind spots are areas in which you remain stubbornly rigid in your views. They prevent you from learning and adapting to change. Obviously, awareness of your blind spots will help you take action to eliminate them on your journey to become a more effective leader.

- **Biases:** Like all human beings—past, present, and future— you are hardwired with innate biases and heuristics (built-in problem-solving routines) that automatically inhibit your otherwise amazingly flawless judgment and decision making. Most of the time these biases and heuristics are so natural that you don't even realize you're using them; and even when you do know, it's hard to change your behavior. What's more, your reasoning becomes imprecise and incomplete, which can lead to distorted views of a situation, incorrect interpretations, inaccurate judgments, and bad decisions. These are detrimental to a leader. Because biases are hardwired, the key here is to become aware of the important ones and put controls in place to minimize their impact.

- **Dominant patterns:** As a leader, you possess unique brain wiring—patterns—that influences your behavior. These deep-seated patterns are filters you use to interact with the world in particular situations. They also shape how you process information and make decisions. These patterns reveal what motivates and demotivates you in a given context (motivation traits), as well as the internal mental processing you use in specific contexts (working traits). Learning to listen for and identify these patterns is key to increasing your understanding of your behavior and that of others. This is powerful stuff for a leader if you can learn to harness it.

- **Moral beliefs and ethical code:** This element of your sight picture addresses the heart of what you stand for in terms of right and wrong (morality) and how you enact those beliefs in your daily leadership walk (ethics). I believe that no other part of your sight picture will have a greater effect on your ability to lead others. Therefore, getting clear on your moral beliefs and ethical code is indispensable.

- **Passions:** Your passions are those feelings that give you effortless energy, enthusiasm, and enjoyment. These are the feelings you experience when you are doing what you really like to do. Passion is a force multiplier when it comes to leadership because it buoys not only your spirit but also the spirit of those you lead.

- **Limiting distortions:** As we all do, you have automatic thought patterns that distort the reality of who you are or the situation in which you find yourself. Bringing these thought patterns to the surface helps eliminate the hold they have over you and allows you to put countermeasures in place. Productively dealing with your limiting distortions paves the way to a healthier self-image and more productive leadership behavior.

- **Professional skills:** Conducting a solid inventory of your technical skills in your functional specialty is important so that you know what your strengths, weaknesses, and gaps are—particularly as they apply to where you are in your career. Part of your credibility as a leader is based on how competent you are in your designated area.

9

- **Resilience:** The demands of your leadership role will place stresses upon you; in order to sustain steady, high-level performance, you must become stress resilient. Lack of stress resilience leads to reductions in performance due to decreases in cognitive intelligence, emotional intelligence, and health. In short, chronic stress is a real danger for you as a leader. When you are stress resilient, you have the capacity and the reserves to productively deal with and manage stress, and thereby avoid catastrophic leadership failure.

- **Capacity for humility and service:** Two of the most important fundamental virtues underlying our view of heroic leadership are humility and service. Being a heroic leader means that you are someone who places your talents and skills, whether large or small, in the service of others. What's more, you serve with an unassuming humility that allows you to fearlessly employ all that you are, while also acknowledging your limitations and others' strengths.

- **Personal mission statement:** Your personal mission statement integrates all that you have learned as part of building your leadership sight picture. It captures your purpose, your vision, who you want to become, and what you intend to accomplish at this particular stage in your leadership journey. Your mission statement helps focus your energy, actions, behaviors, and decisions toward those things that matter most to you as a leader.

★ ★ ★

Once you go through each of these steps, you will (1) have established an exceptionally clear leadership sight picture; (2) know yourself in a much more profound way than you ever have before; and (3) have set the stage for growth, change, and improvement as a heroic leader.

That's powerful!

RECAP

1. Having a clear sight picture keeps you oriented toward your fundamental purpose and goals as a leader.

2. Your leadership sight picture is about self-awareness: knowing who you are, what you stand for, and what makes you tick.

3. Once you establish your personal leadership sight picture, it will set you on the path toward self-mastery.

SELF-COACHING QUESTIONS

1. Of the fifteen elements, which one do you feel is most important to you? Why?

2. Of the fifteen elements, which do you think will require the most work on your part?

3. What are some things you can do to build your leadership sight picture?

INSIGHT #3

It's About "Duty, Honor, Country"
Lead with the Power of Your Values

ON MAY 12, 1962, an aging Douglas MacArthur left his hotel for the United States Military Academy at West Point to accept the Slyvanus Thayer Medal, the highest honor bestowed by the military academy. Little did anyone know that his speech that day would go down as one of the greatest in American history:

> "Duty, honor, country: Those three hallowed words reverently dictate what you ought to be, what you can be, what you will be. They are your rallying point to build courage when courage seems to fail, to regain faith when there seems to be little cause for faith, to create hope when hope becomes forlorn."

MacArthur's speech was about core values, the unassailable principles for which you are responsible and by which you keep the arc of your life on a straight and noble course.

To paraphrase Dr. Martin Luther King Jr., core values comprise the content of your character that provides the spiritual force to your ability to lead. Quite simply, people respond to honest, authentic, and principled leaders.

During my military career, the Air Force adopted the core values of integrity first, service before self, and excellence in all we do. I found that those words served as a constant touchstone for the decisions I made, particularly when I served as judge and jury for disciplinary cases in the units I commanded. I can honestly say they never failed me.

DEEPER INSIGHT

Core values are your unchanging guide for principled behavior and action. They help you discern right from wrong and ensure that your organization remains true to its purpose and mission. In their book *Lies and Truths: Leadership Ethics in the 21st Century,* Nancy Kovanic and Kenneth D. Johnson (2005) wrote: "...individual values are the essence of leadership practices."

Core values provide a basis for interpersonal interaction, group identification, and loyalty. They also form the foundation of your performance, problem solving, and committed effort. Alignment of your values with those of your organization is crucial. Alignment allows you to willingly unleash your energy toward collective goals, while also ensuring that you uphold your values.

According to ethicist Robert Rue, our values are "...the essence of who we are as human beings. Our values get us out of bed every morning, help us select the work we do, the company we keep, the relationships we build, and ultimately, the groups and organizations we lead. Our values influence every decision and move we make, even to the way we choose to make our decisions" (Rue, 2001).

Without core values, people and organizations risk implosion as exemplified by Worldcom, Arthur Anderson, Healthsouth, Enron,

Tyco, and the recent string of Wall Street financial scandals. Core values provide the enduring compass that keeps us on course.

There are several frameworks that can help you discover your core values. One of the most useful frameworks was developed by Shalom Schwartz, a social psychologist and cross-cultural researcher. Schwartz's theory of basic human values identifies ten common values recognized across cultures (Schwartz, 1992). His assessment tool, the Schwartz Values Survey, measures the priority and intensity of these values:

- Self-direction—need for control, mastery, autonomy, and independence
- Stimulation—need for variety and excitement
- Hedonism—need for pleasure and aesthetic beauty
- Achievement—need to demonstrate competence
- Power—need for dominance
- Security—need for safety, harmony, and stability
- Conformity—need to restrain impulses or avoid violating expectations
- Tradition—need for respect, commitment, and acceptance of cultural or religious beliefs and norms of behavior
- Benevolence—concern for the welfare of others
- Universalism—need for understanding, appreciation, tolerance, and protection of people or nature

Another way to understand your personal core values is to start with a list of "master" values and to follow this process:

- Identify all values that you feel are relevant to you personally.
- Rank-order your top five to seven values. In doing so, choose those that apply to your life, help you live out your life purpose, are compatible with the communities and organizations that are important to you, and align with your moral compass.

- Define your top values clearly. For example, if you choose power, what does that word mean to you?

- For each of your top values, make a list of behaviors and attitudes that conform to those values. That way, you will have explicit guidelines for action that are congruent with your top values.

- Implement your core values. In essence, live your life by them.

- Find an accountability partner to help you stay true to your core values.

★ ★ ★

I don't know about you, but I like to sleep well at night knowing that I have stayed true to my values and done my best to do the right thing.

Knowing your values and consistently acting in accordance with them are absolutely necessary to your success as a leader and your ability to lead with authenticity.

RECAP

1. Core values are your unwavering guide for principled behavior and actions.

2. Core values compose the moral essence of who you are as a leader.

3. Core values are the internal compass that keeps you on the straight and true path.

4. It is best when your core values align with those of your organization.

5. There are several frameworks for discovering and assessing your core values; it's important for you to discover what your values are.

6. Knowing your values and consistently acting in accordance with them are critical to your success.

SELF-COACHING QUESTIONS

1. What makes your core values important to you, your people, and your organization?

2. What are the most important core values that underpin your approach to leadership?

3. Are your actions consistent with your core values?

4. What struck you deeply from the core-values discovery process suggested at the end of this chapter? Why?

INSIGHT #4

Washington at Newburgh
Compromise Your Morals, Forfeit Your Right to Lead

"I hope I shall possess firmness and virtue enough
to maintain what I consider the most enviable of all titles,
the character of an honest man."
—*George Washington*

SHORTLY AFTER THE END of the Revolutionary War, the Continental Army was on the verge of insurrection. The core grievance was that neither soldiers nor officers had been paid by Congress.

A group of officers who had gathered at Newburgh, New York, invited George Washington to address their assembly. Their intent was to offer him the position of emperor or even king if he would lead a military coup against the newly founded nation. Washington saw the peril to the new republic for what it was—a direct threat to the country's hard-won liberties.

As Washington stood to address the assembled officers, he slowly pulled a pair of spectacles from his pocket. The room fell suddenly silent, for no one knew the great general required eyeglasses. Even such a simple device to aid the aging Washington was met with disbelief. As he fumbled to adjust his glasses, Washington said, "Gentlemen, you will permit me to put on my spectacles, for I have not only grown gray but nearly blind in the service of my country."

On hearing Washington's words, many in the room broke down in tears. In such a simple act, Washington told those assembled that what they all had fought for was far more precious than whatever grievances they might have. Any thought of a coup was instantly dissolved.

The precedent Washington set ensured that young country would avoid the peril of a military coup. Washington took a moral stand. He acted ethically in the service of the great principles for which the war had been fought. Had he acted differently, a ruinous course would have been set in motion.

Like Washington, you will face moral and ethical challenges throughout your leadership career. Unfortunately, they are unavoidable.

I discovered this all too quickly as a young lieutenant on my first assignment in Germany. I worked for a captain who was having an affair with our married branch chief—a crime under the Uniform Code of Military Justice. What's more, we all worked for a division chief who was discovered smuggling crystal glassware into the country. Eventually, he was fined an entire year's pay.

This kind of behavior was contrary to everything I had been taught about the behavior expected of Air Force officers, not to mention to the way I had been raised.

DEEPER INSIGHT

The cold, hard reality is that moral failures and ethical shortfalls are part of the world we live in. It's not a matter of *if* but of *when* an ethical dilemma will present itself to you.

Not only that you will be faced with multifaceted situations that will challenge your sense of right and wrong. These situations will require you to have a refined moral conscience so that you can discern what's best for your organization and your people. You will be expected to behave ethically despite any pressures placed on you to do otherwise.

Complicating your challenge is that we live in a culture that tilts toward moral relativism—the belief that there is no right or wrong, only a variety of ways to "look at" things. This has created an environment in which many are unwilling to make value judgments. However, leaders are *required* to make such value judgments because of the very nature of their role.

If you aspire to success as a leader, you must be able to reason beyond categories of black and white. Moral reasoning requires nuance. Stepping into the leadership role demands that you make value judgments about the foundational principles that underlie standards of conduct. These judgments inform decision making, which, in turn, precedes ethical conduct and enables moral leadership.

It's easy to preach about ethics but far more difficult to live ethically, especially when you are faced with moral ambiguity.

When it comes to what people expect from their leaders, research in the emerging field of ethical leadership indicates that ethical leaders are thought to be honest, trustworthy, fair, and principled. They are also expected to care about people and the broader community and to conduct their personal and professional lives in a manner consistent with these principles. This is the moral aspect of ethical leadership (Treviño et al., 2000, 2003).

In other words, as an ethical leader, you are expected to "walk the talk." This includes making an effort to positively influence the behavior of those around you by communicating consistent ethical messages, intentionally modeling ethical behavior, and holding people accountable for ethical conduct.

Further, you are responsible for instilling a positive ethical climate in your organization. This responsibility challenges you to answer questions about the kind of climate that you want to permeate your organization.

Such questions include (Thornton, 2006):

- What are the specific ethical behaviors that are required of all organizational leaders?

- What are the consequences for you and your organization if you don't behave ethically?

- What are the situations you may encounter that could lead you into a moral gray area?

- How should you handle these gray areas?

- What does it look like when you perform according to the organization's stated values?

- How should you make decisions when you encounter difficult situations?

- Where might you fall into gray areas as you implement your goals and values?

- In what areas will you not tolerate compromise?

- What are your areas of flexibility?

- Where do you need to clarify your mission and values, to make it apparent that this is an ethical organization, and ethics are not negotiable in an ethical organization?

- How can you more effectively recruit, recognize, and retain ethical leaders?

Ethical culture follows from ethical leadership. It takes leaders who are willing to implement value-based messages, policies, training systems, and personnel-selection processes that support ethical behavior. This approach has been shown to be the most effective in sustaining a morally just, ethically founded organizational culture (Brown & Treviño, 2006).

Also, ethics that are specific to leadership can be developed, especially given the proliferation of university-level courses following the scandal-ridden business history of the past twenty years. These courses share similar structures in that they seek to define the theory and practice of ethical leadership and an ethics-based culture. Methodologies and tools include self-assessments, personal reflection, and feedback, as well as the application of knowledge gained through the use of case studies.

★ ★ ★

You probably will never have to face an imminent coup as Washington did, but you will find yourself dealing with situations that will have far-reaching consequences for the future of your organization. It is your job to make sound decisions, lead with integrity, and build an ethical culture in your organization.

RECAP

1. Moral and ethical behavior is an integral component of leadership.

2. As a leader, you will be faced with situations that will challenge you personally, as well as having significant implications for your organization.

3. Your personal behavior has a direct impact on those around you and the organization.

4. Leaders have a responsibility to instill and sustain an ethical climate in their organizations.

5. Moral judgment and ethical behavior can be taught.

6. It's your job to be morally sound and ethically fit.

SELF-COACHING QUESTIONS

1. What score do you give yourself when it comes to modeling ethical behavior?

2. What does your behavior communicate to others?

3. What moral issues do you anticipate encountering in your leadership role?

4. How well prepared do you think you are for dealing with these issues?

5. Will you have the courage to live out your values when you experience pressure to compromise or rationalize?

6. What can you do to build and strengthen the ethical climate in your organization?

INSIGHT #5

Lead With Superpowers
Leverage Your Strengths

WHAT ARE YOUR SPECIAL SUPERPOWERS—your strengths?

The consensus among leadership experts today is that a strengths-based approach is the most effective way to develop and improve leadership ability.

I learned of one of my strengths when I attended the Naval War College in Newport, Rhode Island, as a young major. The curriculum was tailor-made for me because we were studying history, strategy, and how to create options to meet the national security challenges of our time. I absolutely loved it.

I did well at the school and found that one of my strengths was my ability to envision and create strategy. So after I graduated, I resolved to continue to develop my "strategic chops" and apply my knowledge in future assignments.

Just two years later, I found myself at the Pentagon on the Joint Staff (made up mostly of officers of the Army, Navy, Marine Corps, and Air Force), leading the team charged with writing the first national military strategy for cyberspace operations. I used every bit of what I had learned at the Naval War College to help formulate a viable strategy. It came down to the wire, though: then Secretary Donald Rumsfeld signed the strategy document one day before he left office on December 6, 2006.

The strategy turned out to be a watershed document for the Department of Defense and the armed forces and drove myriad follow-on actions to increase the department's capacity to operate in the cyberspace domain. Although many, many contributors worked to bring that strategy to reality, I was able to use my strength in the area of strategic insight to make a decisive difference.

The point is that your strengths are your special superpowers. You have them for a reason—to use for the betterment of those you lead and the good of the organization.

DEEPER INSIGHT

According to Dr. Martin Seligman (2002), the founder of positive psychology, your strengths:

- Are used in a broad range of situations or settings
- Have a lasting effect over time
- Consistently produce positive outcomes
- Are complementary

The other interesting thing about strengths is that the more of them that you have, the less apparent your weaknesses become.

Strengths can come in many forms: cognitive and emotional intelligence, character virtues, job skills, and expertise. All of these can be accurately identified through assessments, inventories, and performance evaluations. The one I use most often in my consulting practice is the Values in Action (VIA)™ Character Strengths assessment, which rates subjects across twenty-four character strengths that have endured the test of time and have been proven to be valid across all nations and cultures.

These character strengths are as follows:

- **Creativity** [originality, ingenuity]: thinking of novel and productive ways to conceptualize and do things; includes but is not limited to artistic achievement

- **Curiosity** [interest, novelty-seeking, openness to experience]: taking an interest in ongoing experience for its own sake; finding subjects and topics fascinating; exploring and discovering

- **Judgment** [critical thinking]: thinking things through and examining them from all sides; not jumping to conclusions; being able to change one's mind in light of evidence; weighing all evidence fairly

- **Love of learning:** mastering new skills, topics, and bodies of knowledge, whether on one's own or formally; related to but goes beyond curiosity to describe the tendency to add systematically to what one knows

- **Perspective** [wisdom]: providing wise counsel to others; having ways of looking at the world that make sense to oneself and others

- **Bravery** [valor]: not shrinking from threat, challenge, difficulty, or pain; speaking up for what is right even if there is opposition; acting on convictions even when they are unpopular; includes, among other traits, physical bravery

- **Perseverance** [persistence, industriousness]: finishing what one starts; persisting in a course of action in spite of obstacles; "getting it out the door"; taking pleasure in completing tasks

- **Honesty** [authenticity, integrity]: speaking the truth but more broadly presenting oneself in a genuine, sincere way; being without pretense; taking responsibility for one's feelings and actions

- **Zest** [vitality, enthusiasm, vigor, energy]: approaching life with excitement and energy; not doing things halfway or halfheartedly; living life as an adventure; feeling alive and activated

- **Love:** valuing close relationships with others, in particular those in which sharing and caring are reciprocated; being close to people

- **Kindness** [generosity, care, compassion, altruistic love, "niceness"]: doing favors and good deeds for others; helping them; taking care of them

- **Social intelligence** [emotional intelligence, personal intelligence]: being aware of one's motives and feelings as well as those of others; knowing what to do to fit into different social situations; understanding what makes other people tick

- **Teamwork** [citizenship, social responsibility, loyalty]: working well as a member of a group or team; being loyal to the group; doing one's share

- **Fairness:** Treating all people with fairness and justice; not letting personal feelings bias decisions about others; giving everyone a fair chance

- **Leadership:** encouraging a group of which one is a member to get things done while maintaining good relations within the group; organizing group activities and seeing that they happen

- **Forgiveness:** forgiving those who have done wrong; accepting the shortcomings of others; giving people a second chance; not being vengeful

- **Humility:** letting one's accomplishments speak for themselves; not regarding oneself as particularly special

- **Prudence:** being careful about one's choices; not taking undue risks; not saying or doing things that might later be regretted

- **Self-regulation** [self-control]: regulating what one feels and does; being disciplined; controlling appetites and emotions

- **Appreciation of beauty and excellence** [awe, wonder, elevation]: noticing and appreciating beauty, excellence, and skilled performance in various domains of life, from mathematics and science to art and everyday experience

- **Gratitude:** being aware of and thankful for the good things that happen; taking time to express thanks

- **Hope** [optimism, future-mindedness, future orientation]: expecting the best in the future and working to achieve it; believing that positive things can happen

- **Humor** [playfulness]: liking to laugh and tease; bringing smiles to other people; seeing the light side; making jokes

- **Spirituality** [faith, purpose]: having coherent beliefs about the higher purpose and meaning of the universe; knowing where one fits within the larger scheme; having beliefs about the meaning of life that shape conduct and provide comfort

Once you identify your strengths, the good news is that they can be developed and enhanced. The research clearly shows that "strengthening your strengths" will make you a better leader, objectively, in terms of your ability to lead, and subjectively, in the eyes of those who see you lead.

★ ★ ★

Your signature strengths are assets that enable you to lead from a place of genuineness and personal power. The key is to make the commitment to build them. Like the pursuit of all worthwhile things, that takes practice, effort, and determination.

RECAP

1. A strengths-based approach is an effective way to build your leadership ability.

2. Strengths are your special "superpowers" that enable you to lead confidently and competently.

3. Strengths can be learned and developed.

4. Amplifying your strengths diminishes any weaknesses you might have.

5. There are a number of assessments to help you identify your strengths.

6. Like all worthwhile endeavors, building your strengths takes time, effort, and determination.

SELF-COACHING QUESTIONS

1. What are my signature strengths?

2. How do I use my strengths to empower my people and build my organization?

3. How have my strengths helped me in past and present leadership roles?

4. What can I do to build and enhance my strengths?

INSIGHT #6

Powell, Rumsfeld, or Wooden?
Base Your Leadership Success on a Great Model

DURING HIS MILITARY CAREER, Colin Powell had his "Thirteen Rules of Leadership." One of my favorites was, "Perpetual optimism is a force multiplier."

Secretary of Defense Donald Rumsfeld was known for his Rumsfeld's Rules, such as "If you are working from your inbox, you are working on other people's priorities."

John Wooden had his "Rules to Lead By," which resulted in seven consecutive NCAA basketball championships. A key rule for him was, "Be more concerned with your character than your reputation. Character is what you really are. Reputation is what people say you are. Character is more important."

These lists of rules were essentially a distillation of the leadership models of these three successful leaders. As a young Air Force officer, I always found such lists useful, but it wasn't until later that I was finally able to formulate my own distinct approach.

Now it's time for you to come up with yours.

The problem is that there are so many leadership models out there, it's difficult to settle on one. In addition to the models of great leaders, the models that have resulted from academic research include the following:

- Great man theory
- Trait theory
- Attribute pattern theory
- Expectancy theory
- Situational leadership
- Contingency leadership
- Functional leadership
- Relational leadership
- Transactional leadership
- Charismatic leadership
- Transformational leadership
- Authentic leadership
- Values-based leadership
- Ethical leadership
- Servant leadership
- Crisis leadership

Your leadership model ultimately must be a product of your own experience, training, and education. As you continue to lead, the key is to learn, refine, select, and incorporate leadership models in order to create the most effective one for you at the current stage of your leadership journey.

The way you operate as a leader is influenced by who you are and what you stand for (your leadership sight picture); your background, training, and education; your organizational culture; and your culture of origin. As such, your personal leadership model serves to guide the way you lead.

DEEPER INSIGHT

Given this approach, here's something important to consider: You have a leadership model whether or not you know you do. Wouldn't it be better to be *explicit* about your leadership model so that *you* control it rather than letting *it* control you? The great thing is that your personal journey is like one huge leadership laboratory. You will encounter both good and bad leaders, read books, take courses, and gain experience—all of which, bit by bit, will leave a mark on you. What this means it that you will have ample opportunity to develop a model that works for you—one that you consciously construct.

A model provides a touchstone for you as you proceed on your leadership journey. Your model will help keep you from being buffeted by current fads and external pressures.

As my own leadership model developed, I relied less on examples of leadership and more on proven academic research that matched my own personal experience. During the last few years of my career as a leader, it seemed that I learned more about leadership than I had in the previous ten. I wish I had known earlier much of what I learned later. Nonetheless, I made the adjustments, improved on my model, and became a more effective leader.

I continue to learn and refine my leadership model. I find this to be a never-ending and exciting challenge.

By way of example, at The Leadership Crucible, we base our leadership approach on a synthesis of the best research and thinking on the subject, personal experience, and expert counsel. The most significant models we use include the following:

Servant Leadership: Robert Greenleaf started the servant-leadership revolution with an essay he published in 1970 called "The Servant as Leader." Greenleaf held that a servant-leader fundamentally thinks less of self than of others, shares power, develops people, and works to help them perform to their potential.

Leader-Member Exchange Theory (LMX): Developed in the early 1970s, LMX has been well researched in the ensuing forty years. Its basic tenet is that leaders generate more effective leadership if they develop and maintain mature relationships. LMX gets at questions of leader support of followers and follower trust of leaders. The stronger the relationship between leaders and followers, the better the results.

Transformational Leadership: James MacGregor Burns (1978), a presidential historian, first described transformational leadership in his book *Leadership*. Burns defined this leadership style as one in which "leaders and followers help each other to advance to a higher level of morale and motivation." An additional thirty-plus years of research have yielded four key elements of transformational leadership:

- *Individualized consideration* is how much the leader takes care of the concerns and needs of the followers.
- *Intellectual stimulation* refers to the leader who encourages independent thinking and creativity in followers.
- *Inspirational motivation* means that the leader develops a shared vision that inspires the team to high levels of commitment and performance.
- *Idealized influence* is the way leaders model the behavior they expect of others.

Kouzes and Posner's *Five Practices of Exemplary Leadership* (1987) is a practical application of transformational leadership. It is a very effective model for new leaders, and it is one that I use in my coaching practice.

Level-5 Leadership: Level-5 Leadership was first articulated by Jim Collins (2001) in his book *Good to Great*. Collins's research revealed that an indispensable requirement for a great company is an executive who exhibits genuine personal humility blended with intense professional will. Recall that humility is also essential for the type of leadership I have described in this book.

Strengths-based Leadership: Based on the positive-psychology movement begun by Dr. Martin Seligman in 1998, this model uses psychological theory to understand the emotionally fulfilling aspects of human behavior. As a product of his research, Seligman identified twenty-four timeless, cross-cultural strengths common to the human experience (as described in Insight #5). By employing your strengths, you increase your chances of living a happier, more fulfilled life.

Zenger and Folkman (2009) discovered that a leader who has two or three outstanding leadership-related strengths is perceived to be "extraordinary." They recommend growing the "strength of your strengths" and improving critical weaknesses to be successful as a leader.

Flexible Leadership: Dr. Gary Yukl has taught and written about leadership for the better part of forty years. In addition to writing many seminal articles on leadership over the years, Yukl authored the book *Flexible Leadership*. Flexible leadership is a comprehensive theory that "integrates findings from different disciplines and more than a half-century of research and explains how leaders can effectively enhance the bottom-line performance of their organizations" (Yukl & Lepsinger, 2004). This grounded, practical approach makes it particularly useful for leadership training.

Three Levels of Leadership: The 3P model (Scouller, 2010), as it is known, stands for public, private, and personal leadership. Public leadership applies to group leadership and the functions of establishing purpose, accomplishing tasks, and maintaining group unity. Private leadership is one-on-one leadership and focuses on individual accomplishment of tasks and taking care of people. Personal leadership is self-mastery and encompasses the leader's presence, expert knowledge, and people skills. Scouller maintains that self-mastery is the basis for any success a leader might experience. Among its many merits, Scouller's model emphasizes the psychological aspect of leadership.

★ ★ ★

Your leadership model is the mental map that guides and directs the way you go about leading. As such, it is vitally important to actively improve your model as you continue on your leadership journey. Although you might end up taking a few thoughts from Powell, Rumsfeld, or Wooden, the idea is not to copy them but to formulate your own model that fits your personal leadership sight picture.

RECAP
1. Whether or not you realize it, you have an implicit leadership model that underlies and guides your approach to leadership.
2. It's better to make this model explicit so that you control it rather than having it control you.
3. Your leadership model will continue to develop and change as your experience, training, and formal learning change over time.
4. There are many academic models of leadership. It's worth exploring them to select the ones that resonate with you for incorporation into your personal model.

SELF-COACHING QUESTIONS

1. What is your current leadership model?

2. How did your leadership model develop?

3. What are the most important elements of your model?

4. What does your current leadership role require of you?

5. Does your leadership model allow you to fulfill this role in an exemplary way?

6. What are some things you can do to improve on your leadership model?

INSIGHT #7

"I Do Solemnly Swear to Support and Defend"
Do You Pass the Buck or Accept the Blame?

"I do solemnly swear that I will support and defend the
Constitution of the United States against all enemies, foreign
and domestic; that I will bear true faith and allegiance to the
same; that I take this obligation freely, without any mental
reservation or purpose of evasion; and that I will well and
faithfully discharge the duties of the office upon which
I am about to enter; so help me God."
—*Armed Forces Oath of Office for Officers*

MILITARY OFFICERS TAKE THIS OATH OF OFFICE when they are
commissioned and reaffirm it at every subsequent promotion. It
is indeed a solemn oath and an equally solemn responsibility that
animates everything officers do from the moment they repeat
those words.

In swearing allegiance to the US Constitution—not to a person
or a political party—the officer affirms the basis of leadership
accountability in support of the higher principles that guided this
country to its freedom.

I recall May 19, 1989, the day I was commissioned, as clearly as if it were yesterday. Not only was it the achievement of a goal I had set for myself five years earlier while I was in high school, it was also the beginning of an exciting new career in serving my country. I took my oath with a tremendous sense of responsibility and commitment. Later, I had my commissioning certificate framed and hung it over my desk at every new assignment to remind me of the promise I had made. It still hangs in my office today.

Later in my career, I learned the full meaning of accountability as I was assigned as commander of five progressively larger units. When I was given the unit flag that symbolized the leadership role I had over the unit on the day I took command, I could feel the weight of responsibility settle on my shoulders. If anything went wrong—as it inevitably would, of course—I would be the one who would be called on the carpet.

DEEPER INSIGHT

Accountability is an internal sense of ownership of (1) the responsibilities you are assigned as a leader and (2) the results you are responsible for producing. Accountability also assumes a certain moral obligation on your part to perform your duties to the best of your ability.

Being accountable means that you are willing to submit your actions to the judgment of others. You are prepared to explain or justify your opinions, intentions, acts, and omissions when called to do so. These include any errors, misjudgments, or negligence. When things go well, being accountable means that you accept the acknowledgment of your competence and conscientiousness. No matter what happens, accountability signals your willingness to change for the better in light of others' evaluations.

When you say you are accountable, you mean:

- I am responsible.
- I am willing to be held to standards.
- I work to produce the results expected of me—and more, if I can.
- I admit when I am wrong.
- I own failure when it happens.
- I don't assign blame; I look in the mirror.
- I act in accordance with my organization's values and vision.

President Harry Truman's famous sign on his desk read, "The buck stops here," clearly indicating where accountability lay. In contrast, "passing the buck" characterizes people who rationalize, create excuses, blame others, procrastinate, complain, and do the minimum. They say things such as:

- I didn't know.
- I wasn't there.
- I don't have time.
- It's not my job.
- That's just the way I am.
- Nobody told me.
- It isn't really hurting anyone.
- I'm just following orders.

★　★　★

Lack of accountability is like a highly contagious disease within an organization and invites disaster such as we witnessed with Enron and Abu Ghraib. When all is said and done, accountability may very well be the fundamental aspect of heroic leadership: the individual's willing acceptance of responsibility to a higher purpose, a commitment to produce expected results, and a readiness to be judged on personal behavior and results.

RECAP

1. Being accountable means you accept your responsibilities as a leader.
2. It also means that you accept the consequences if your leadership does not produce the results for which you are answerable.
3. Accountability is a crucial ingredient for success as a leader.

SELF-COACHING QUESTIONS

1. Are you fully accountable for the results under your control, whether things go well or badly?
2. In what instances have you demonstrated accountability?
3. What stands out in your mind about the times when you failed to be accountable for your decisions, actions, or outcomes?
4. What did you learn from those experiences?

INSIGHT #8

Of Generals and Admirals
Work Incessantly to Achieve Leadership Mastery

"The hardest victory is the victory over self."
—*Aristotle*

DURING MY AIR FORCE CAREER, I had the opportunity to work for many senior officers who held the rank of general or admiral. What was amazing to me was not only how exceptional they all were but also how hard they worked. In fact, it is my opinion that our generals and admirals are some of the hardest-working leaders anywhere, especially when you take into account that they are responsible for implementing our nation's defensive capabilities, sometimes under very trying conditions. The conflicts in Iraq and Afghanistan are only two examples.

For these remarkable leaders to have risen to such lofty ranks was an extended process over many years. It included depth and breadth of job responsibilities, a wide variety of experiences, progressive education, and yes, the crucible of conflict. Even after they reached general or flag rank, they continued to attend executive leadership courses and to take advantage of mentorship and coaching. The growth and hard work never end.

Perhaps most important, these senior leaders immersed themselves in the art and science of leadership until it became as natural to them as breathing. And without a doubt, all along the way, they worked incessantly to achieve leadership mastery.

DEEPER INSIGHT

The road to mastery is part and parcel of your leadership crucible. What we're talking about here is top-echelon mastery—not only being among the very best at what you do but also being the very best you can *be*.

Mastery requires incredible commitment, struggle, and sacrifice. You must stay true to your intent year after year, constantly pushing beyond the edge of your abilities. As soon as you establish a new benchmark for achievement, you must strive to establish an even higher one.

According to leadership expert James Scouller (2010), there are three basic components of leadership mastery: technical skill, attitude toward others, and self-mastery.

Technical skill: This is your stock in trade as a leader. It is the reason you attend school. Technical skill includes functional knowledge, general knowledge, and strategic knowledge.

- *Functional knowledge* includes the principles and methods of your organization and its components, such as accounting practices, manufacturing processes, and administration.

- *General knowledge* is knowledge of your industry, what makes your customers tick, budgeting, and project management.

- *Strategic knowledge* applies to organizational change and anticipation of opportunities and threats to your organization or industry.

Without solid technical skill, it will be difficult—if not impossible—to achieve leadership mastery because you won't be perceived as credible at what you do. In addition, you will need to keep yourself continually updated on your functional-area expertise in order to stay current with the latest developments in your field.

Attitude toward others: Leadership is about your team's and your ability to produce the results required for success. If you are going to get these results, your people must accept you as a credible leader. For this to happen, you need to (1) treat them with respect and dignity, (2) put the collective interest of the team above your own interest, (3) tell the truth, and (4) follow through on your promises.

Your attitude toward others has mental, emotional, and behavioral elements. For example, you and the members of your team are interdependent. It is up to you to genuinely appreciate and care for them as you elevate them to higher levels of performance.

To get an idea of how important respect, collective interest, truth telling, and "walking your talk" are to your role as a leader, just think of someone you worked for who did not display these characteristics. Did you respect that leader? How hard did you work for that person? If you answered the questions as most people do, the connection between attitude, credibility, and performance should be clear: the less credible the leader, the poorer the performance of the rest of the team. Your attitude toward others has a decisive impact on your ability to lead.

Self-mastery: Being the best you can be involves the pursuit of self-mastery in addition to the functional skills acquired through deliberate practice. Self-mastery refers to the all-important inner game of leadership. It requires a high degree of self-awareness and firm command of your mind.

To achieve self-mastery, you must let go of limiting beliefs and ingrained habits. Once these beliefs and habits have been swept away, you will find yourself more closely aligned with your core values, which will allow your authentic leadership presence to be revealed.

In *The Three Levels of Leadership*, Scouller (2011) explains that self-mastery:

- Allows you to express your authentic presence that makes others want to follow you.

- Focuses your energies, enabling you to achieve more, with greater efficiency.

- Increases your ability to handle pressure and get into the "flow" of leadership, giving you a sense of ease and enjoyment.

- Dissolves your limiting beliefs, improves your self-image, and raises your self-esteem.

You attain these benefits by steady, "inside-out" efforts. If you want to make progress, Scouller recommends several keys:

- **Set goals along the way.** Provide yourself with a concrete objective so that you will move forward.

- **Focus on what you can control.** Understand that you have control over your choices and reactions no matter what has triggered your responses in the past.

- **Uncover your limiting beliefs.** Identify those dominant habits of thought that underpin your behavior and hold you back. Use this awareness to consciously choose your behavior rather than reverting to old patterns.

- **Be open to learning.** As you make progress, you must be willing to continue to grow.

- **Have the humility to ask for help.** Understand that the journey to self-mastery is tough to complete on your own. Others can assist you along the way as long as you are willing to accept their help.

In order to develop the three basic components of self-mastery to a highly refined level, you need a structure to help direct your efforts. K. Anders Ericsson (2007), a pioneer researcher on excellence, outlined three elements of self-mastery: deliberate practice, expert coaching, and a support system.

Deliberate practice: In *The Road to Excellence: The Acquisition of Expert Performance in the Arts and Sciences, Sports, and Games,* K. Anders Ericsson (1996) was the first to write an in-depth description of the importance of deliberate practice in the pursuit of elite performance in diverse disciplines such as chess, violin playing, and track and field. Malcolm Gladwell (2009) later popularized this notion when he observed that it takes "ten thousand hours" to achieve mastery.

Since then, however, the idea of ten thousand hours has become trivialized beyond recognition. It is common sense that if anyone spends ten thousand hours doing anything, he will most likely get passably good at it. However, to achieve mastery requires more time spent practicing.

Ericsson and his colleagues shed more light on the type of practiced required:

> "When most people practice, they focus on the things they already know how to do. Deliberate practice is different. It entails considerable, specific, and sustained efforts to

do something you can't do well—or even at all. Research across domains shows that it is only by working at what you can't do that you turn into the expert you want to become" (Ericsson, Prietula & Cokely, 2007).

To practice deliberately according to Ericsson (2007), means:

- You focus on the task at hand and put forth effort to improve.

- The task should be just difficult enough to stretch you beyond your previous level of competence.

- You receive prompt, helpful feedback on how you did on the task.

- You repeat the task until you achieve proficiency.

When applied to leadership, this kind of deliberate practice is more difficult due to the multilayered nature of the leader's environment. However, it is certainly not impossible. Case studies, war games, and emergency-scenario rehearsals all provide opportunities to stretch capabilities, receive feedback, and hone newly acquired skills.

Expert coaching: Think of any professional athlete, singer, musician, or actor, and you will realize the importance of high-quality coaching. We're talking about coaching that is closely supervised, hard hitting, and tough. As Ericsson and his colleagues observed:

"If we analyze the development of the well-known artists, we see that in almost every case the success of their entire career was dependent on the quality of their practicing. In practically every case, the practicing was constantly supervised either by the teacher or an assistant to the teacher" (Ericsson, Prietula & Cokely, 2007).

Coaches are indispensable in identifying areas of improvement and for pushing you beyond your boundaries so that you can rise to higher levels of excellence.

Support system: To get to the very highest echelon in your field, you must surround yourself with a cadre of people who support you in your efforts. This includes family, friends, and those you hire (including coaches). These are the people who will be there for you with a good word when times are tough, and there will be many such times along this journey.

★ ★ ★

Leadership mastery is neither an overnight process nor an easy one. It takes years of steady effort to make progress. It involves acquiring new technical skills, developing an attitude of service to others, and the difficult inner work of self-mastery. You need to engage in deliberate practice under the watchful eye of a coach and build a support system of people to help you along the way.

But the rewards of leadership mastery far exceed the price, especially when you realize the positive impact you will have on the people around you—and the world.

RECAP
1. Leadership mastery requires:
   - Sustained commitment, struggle, and sacrifice
   - Technical skill and an attitude of service toward others
   - Self-mastery
   - Deliberate practice, expert coaching, and a support system

2. Your progress toward leadership mastery ultimately depends on you—your commitment, your determination, and your willingness to learn.

SELF-COACHING QUESTIONS

1. How do you rate your current level of leadership mastery?

2. How would others rate you?

3. How committed are you to achieving leadership mastery?

4. Do you engage in deliberate practice? If so, do you do it every day?

5. Do you have a leadership coach?

6. Whom do you consider to be part of your support system?

7. Is your support system actually supportive? How so?

INSIGHT #9

Win the War!
Create and Implement Your Campaign Strategy

"The one who adapts his policy to the times prospers,
and likewise the one whose policy clashes
with the demands of the times does not."
—*Machiavelli*

WITH A NOD TO MACHIAVELLI, in military parlance, a campaign is a large-scale, long-term plan designed to achieve a specified, high-level outcome, usually related to national priorities (e.g., expel Saddam Hussein's forces from Kuwait).

A campaign strategy is the overall orchestrating concept and design for the armed forces to achieve the desired end state in support of national policy. The campaign strategy organizes, aligns, and orchestrates military action toward that desired end state.

The point here for leaders is that you need an overarching strategy to achieve your organizational, professional, and personal goals. Without one, it's like being adrift on the ocean without a sail or a compass: You're at the mercy of the winds and the currents, and there is very little chance that you will reach your intended destination.

As a five-time commander in the Air Force, I adapted the idea of constructing a campaign plan to implementation of a strategy my team and I had developed for the two-year period of my command assignment. I found that, as our strategy and plan were pulled together, they had a galvanizing effect on everyone in the organization. Everyone knew the part he needed to play to make the entire organization successful, which was valuable in and of itself.

Even with a strategy, the process toward your desired end state will at times be difficult. As Karl von Clausewitz (1832), a Prussian general and the author of the classic military text, *On War*, said, "In war, even the easiest things are difficult."

As a military commander, I found von Clausewitz's words to be true. Although I had tremendous authority over my units, our success still required all the skill, savvy, and determination I could muster—especially when facing unexpected challenges, external resistance, and the political gamesmanship that comes with moving a campaign forward.

DEEPER INSIGHT

A strategy keeps your goals top of mind and provides a "war-winning" template to help you stay on course and address the challenges that will surely come your way. For my part, I had no doubt that the campaigns my team and I built provided the focus we needed to move forward and judge our progress.

Good leaders will ask themselves several questions to elicit reflection about the organization's strategy. These include:

- **Who are we?** This question gets to the type of values, ethos, culture, style, and aspirations that form the essence and foundation of your organization.

- **Where are we now?** This leads to a comprehensive assessment of your organization's mission as it applies to your competitive environment. To answer this question, you must:
  - ‣ Understand stakeholder expectations and customer needs
  - ‣ Clarify your core competencies
  - ‣ Assess your resources and processes
  - ‣ Pinpoint internal strengths and weaknesses
  - ‣ Identify external opportunities and threats

  This information will help you see gaps, issues, and challenges you need to deal with in order to accomplish your mission and organizational vision.

- **Where do we want to go?** In this step, you use the assessment of your organization's mission (see above) to develop your overarching strategy and campaign plan. The elements of this step include:
  - ‣ Revising your vision
  - ‣ Selecting your internal and external priorities
  - ‣ Delineating the focus of your main efforts and the scope of those efforts
  - ‣ Comparing options
  - ‣ Assessing risk

  Place significant emphasis on the ways, means, and resources you need to achieve the goals of the campaign plan.

- **How do we get there?** Here, you execute your campaign plan using well-defined goals that also answer the who, what, when, where, why, and how (W5H) questions. You then put in motion the means of achieving your objectives, overcoming resistance and friction, increasing trust, and empowering your people. Your task is to ensure that processes, policies, structure, and technology are aligned to move you toward achieving your goals.

- **Are we getting there?** This step identifies control systems, diagnostics, performance drivers, and metrics that will track progress. It also distinguishes outputs and outcomes, leading and lagging indicators, efficiency and effectiveness, and belief and boundary systems.

Asking good questions about the organization's strategy drives deep reflection and wide-ranging discussion to generate insight, ideas, and consensus on a viable, measurable way forward for the organization. The questions elicit meaningful conversation related to the changes in the competitive environment, how these changes affect the organization, how the organization intends to deal with them, and how the organization can benefit from them. The result is a tangible strategy that can be used to move in a unified, deliberate manner toward the future your leadership team has envisioned.

Done well, a campaign strategy:

- Allows you to take control of your own destiny
- Crystallizes goals
- Establishes priorities
- Provides focus
- Channels effort and energy
- Capitalizes on what you do well or the organization does well
- Serves as a rallying point for commitment and engagement
- Optimizes your (or the organization's) potential
- Aligns resources and support
- Drives concrete results

★ ★ ★

A well-conceived, well-executed campaign plan increases the potential not only for the survival of a leader or an organization, but more important, for the achievement of growth, success, and prosperity.

RECAP

1. A campaign strategy is the overall orchestrating concept to achieve goals in support of an organization's mission.

2. A campaign strategy can also be applied to a leader's professional or personal goals.

3. A campaign strategy provides an enduring touchstone to keep leaders and their organizations focused on the desired end state, especially when the going gets tough.

4. Use a deliberate method to systematically put together your campaign strategy.

5. A well-constructed campaign strategy increases your chances of professional, personal, and organizational success.

SELF-COACHING QUESTIONS

1. What is your professional campaign strategy? What is your organization's strategy?

2. How are they working? How do you know if they are working and how effective they are? What weaknesses, if any, have you identified?

3. What can you do to improve your campaign planning process?

4. What can you do to improve the implementation of your campaign strategy?

INSIGHT #10

Intelligence, Surveillance, and Reconnaissance
Sense the Competitive Environment

THERE IS NO MORE high-stakes, competitive environment than war. Within this cauldron of violence and destruction, astute military leaders have long attempted to use every means at their disposal to find out as much about the enemy and the battlefield as possible. They gather intelligence, conduct surveillance, and perform reconnaissance in order to gain whatever advantage they can over the adversary—and equally important, to avoid surprise, losses, and catastrophe. Sensing the present and future events that transpire in war is essential to have any chance of winning one.

From a military standpoint, sensing occurs through the employment of intelligence, surveillance, and reconnaissance (ISR) platforms and processes. Think spy satellites, U-2 aircraft, drones, undercover agents, and intelligence reports.

From an aerial point of view, the first operational use of fixed-wing aircraft was for a reconnaissance mission. The flight took place in 1911 during the Italo-Turkish War when an Italian Blériot XI aircraft scouted Turkish positions near Benghazi.

Fast-forward to the Korean War when a confident fighter pilot named John Boyd began to think hard about how to win jet-on-jet dogfights. He not only thought about it, he became very good at doing it. After the war, while teaching at the US Air Force's elite Fighter Weapons School, he was known as "40-second Boyd." This was a reference to his ability to outmaneuver an opposing jet that had settled in on his "six"—the highly vulnerable rear of his aircraft—and reverse their positions.

Out of this crucible of war and realistic training, Boyd (1976) originated his now-famous Observe-Orient-Decide-Act (OODA) loop concept in which he asserted that all intelligent organisms (that would include leaders!) and organizations undergo a continuous cycle of interaction with their environment. Boyd believed that those who continually create and exploit competitive advantage have the best chance of surviving and prospering.

As a leader, part of your job is to make sure that you have the most accurate picture possible of your operating environment. You do this through the process of observation.

DEEPER INSIGHT

Observation is a critical but often overlooked and underappreciated process of collecting information from your surrounding environment and paying attention to how circumstances are unfolding.

Observation is an ongoing assessment of opportunities, threats, and actions emerging around you that allows you to establish a baseline of accurate situational awareness. With this information in hand, you are better prepared to position yourself for success, decide what to do, and take actions that lead to the results you seek.

Visualize a football quarterback reading the defense before the ball is snapped. A quarterback scans the field to gather information about formations, alignments, and matchups. He then uses that information to adjust his own formation, call the signals, and align the offensive to achieve an advantage once the ball is in play.

From a leadership standpoint, comprehensive and accurate observation allows you to understand the strategic context in which you must operate. This task is made even more difficult because a leader's environment is often not only competitive but also volatile, uncertain, and ambiguous.

Nonetheless, it is imperative to be on the lookout for new information that adds to, enhances, and deepens your understanding of your environment. The more relevant information you can reliably take in, the more accurate your understanding will be. Just like Boyd, the fighter pilot, you want to be scanning the horizon for enemy aircraft, monitoring the performance of your jet, and preparing to decide and act on what you know.

Observations can originate from data, test results, analysis of the competition, models, customer feedback, metrics, your team, and what you yourself gather. Questions you should ask to help you sense the competitive environment are:

- What's happening in the environment that directly affects us?
- What's happening that indirectly affects us?
- What's happening that may have residual effects later on?
- Were our predictions accurate?
- Are there any areas where prediction and reality differ significantly?

A leader who successfully observes the environment, senses what is happening, and understands what is important for the organization to deal with places the survival and prosperity of the organization on firm footing.

★ ★ ★

Without the good situational awareness provided by ISR, as Boyd said, "We will find it impossible to comprehend, shape, adapt to, and in turn be shaped by an unfolding, evolving reality." That reality, according to Boyd, "is uncertain, ever-changing, and unpredictable."

And as a leader, that is your reality, too.

RECAP

1. Part of your job is to make sure you have as accurate a picture as possible of your operating environment.

2. You do this through the process of observation.

3. By observing the environment, you gather the information through ISR that allows you to assess the opportunities, threats, and actions transpiring around you.

4. Comprehensive and accurate observation allows you to understand the strategic context in which you must operate.

5. Observations can originate from a variety of sources. The point is to continually collect information so that you can update, improve, and enhance your situational awareness.

SELF-COACHING QUESTIONS

1. How well do you observe your operational environment?

2. What techniques or methods work best for you in observing your environment?

3. What are your data sources?

4. How accurate and reliable are they?

5. How can you tell if you've missed anything? How do you cross-check what you think you know?

6. What processes and systems do you have in place to help you sense the competitive environment?

INSIGHT #11

Stirrups, Airplanes, and Radios
You Must Deal With Change

"The only thing harder than getting a new idea
into the military mind is to get an old one out."
—*B. H. Liddell Hart,* Thoughts on War*, 1944*

THE STORY OF WARFARE is inextricably tied to technological
change.

For example, the Mongols mastered the stirrup, which enabled
their cavalry to become much more accurate with arrow, spear, and
sword. This gave their riders a tremendous tactical advantage over
opposing armies and contributed to the vast Mongol conquests
during the Middle Ages.

Similarly, during World War I, both sides realized the value of
the airplane, first for artillery ranging and surveillance and then
for aerial bombardment. By the end of the war, vast armadas of
aircraft were clashing in the air and raining destruction on armies,
supply lines, and cities.

The radio was initially used during World War I but came into its own in World War II when the Germans used it to integrate ground, air, and armor forces into their blitzkrieg operations. Radios allowed commanders to be in instant contact with headquarters, support units, and field troops, resulting in enhanced situational awareness, faster decision making, more rapid and improved massing of force, and—especially at the outset of the war—more decisive engagements.

The real lesson about technological change is that it is emblematic of the need for organizations to adapt to the dynamic competitive environment. An organization that fails to do this begins to lose market share and hemorrhage talent. As time goes on, without making the necessary adjustments, the organization falls further and further behind and eventually goes out of business.

DEEPER INSIGHT

The main point for leaders is that use of technology is inevitable in the ongoing search for a competitive advantage, whether in warfare or in business. If you want to remain viable and relevant, you are compelled to adopt new technology.

Even more important is the notion that change is part of the broader scientific enterprise with its built-in method of expanding knowledge.

Finally, and more fundamentally, change is inherent in the Western philosophical ethic of progress, which holds that we can improve society and ourselves.

What this ethic has produced is unremitting, accelerated rates of change fueled by free-market capitalism and hyper-consumption. This state of affairs makes it difficult for leaders to stay on top of changes that affect their organizations, make forward-thinking decisions, and move ahead with any kind of certainty.

Keeping all this in mind, let's take another look at military strategist John Boyd's OODA loop (the process by which an individual or an organization reacts and adapts to an event) and how it can assist a leader in dealing with change.

Boyd (1992) viewed reality itself as a process of ceaseless change that unfolds "in an irregular, disorderly, unpredictable manner." In his view, "We must continue the whirl of reorientation, mismatches, analysis, and synthesis over and over again ad infinitum."

What Boyd was saying is that in order to deal with change successfully, you must continually update your map of reality with new information, test it, and then update it again when you find your map to be inaccurate, out of date, or lacking. If not, you automatically accept the risk and responsibility of leading your organization into obsolescence and irrelevance.

Leaders must observe and orient to change and then make decisions and act. This requires a specific skill set that allows you to:

- See connections between external trends and relate those trends to the core mission of the organization
- Establish an organizational culture that embraces change
- Facilitate innovation
- Create an organization that thrives on challenges
- Communicate a shared vision of change in clear language
- Influence attitudes toward change
- Develop and monitor metrics that measure response to change
- Recognize and reward change-driven behavior and results
- Face resistance to change directly and courageously
- Provide the resources, time, and money to support change-based initiatives
- Inculcate a bias toward change in suppliers, consumer behavior, industry norms, and government policy

- Engage diverse stakeholders and partners in a broad-based effort to implement a change-oriented infrastructure supported by policy, legal frameworks, processes, and technology

The last major cavalry charge occurred during World War II. In 1942, a regiment of six hundred Italian horsemen conducted the last significant horse-mounted attack against well-entrenched Soviet infantrymen. The attack against machine guns and mortars was costly, but it was effective at dislodging the Soviets from their positions.

The irony should not be lost that the Italians had been the first to use the aircraft in conflict forty years earlier; yet, they and most of the other combatants had horse cavalry at the outset of World War II.

★ ★ ★

In today's change-driven society, you can ill afford to be sluggish about change. Rather, as Boyd's OODA loop model demonstrates, the key to surviving and thriving is not only your ability to adapt to change but also to lead it.

RECAP

1. Technology is emblematic of change but is only one part of the broader context of change in our contemporary society.
2. Change is inevitable, but the Western ethic of scientific progress, coupled with market-driven capitalism, has increased the speed at which change occurs.
3. Leaders ignore this dynamic at their own and their organizations' risk.
4. As a continually updating, learning, and experiential process, John Boyd's OODA loop provides an effective model to help leaders deal with change.

5. Leading change requires a specific skill set that cuts across multiple domains of expertise.

6. The key to surviving and thriving in a rapidly changing environment is to adapt to it, as well as to lead it.

SELF-COACHING QUESTIONS

1. What is your attitude toward change in your personal or professional life?

2. How comfortable are you when change occurs?

3. Recall a time when you successfully led an organization, especially your current one, through a major change. What were the circumstances? How did it turn out? What did you learn? What would you do differently?

4. What skills do you have to lead change? What skills do you need?

5. How open (or resistant) to change is your organization? How do you know?

6. How well has your organization dealt with or capitalized on change in the past? Describe the situation.

INSIGHT #12

Power from the Edge
Leverage the Field for Innovation

THE LARGER AND MORE SET in its ways an organization becomes, the more difficult it is to bring about innovation. Things get even more difficult when innovation is not built into the organizational DNA, and the culture is unable to promote free exchange and implementation of new ideas.

One of the most powerful lessons I ever learned as a young Air Force officer was when I went on my first deployment in support of NATO air operations over Bosnia-Herzegovina. Prior to the deployment I had worked in communications-engineering jobs that were highly regulated by process and hierarchy. Stability and predictability were prized; new and innovative ideas and approaches were not.

On my arrival at the theater air operations center—the nerve center for the air war—as the chief of communications engineering, I quickly discovered that my chain of command to the three-star general in charge was incredibly short. There was only one layer between the general and me. The second thing I realized was there were no manuals or regulations that stipulated what I was to do. The basic guidance was something like, "Make sure everything we have keeps working, but do everything you can to improve it."

This was my first experience with the freedom to innovate, and I felt as if I had been reborn. For me, the experience was liberating.

Even more energizing was that the team of airmen deployed there as communications technicians was renowned for its ability to solve problems and find creative ways to meet operational demands. In time, I was able to gain the trust of these airmen. Together, we not only kept everything working but also implemented a variety of first-ever communications networks, relays, and connections that enhanced the ability of the three-star NATO commander and his field commanders to conduct air operations over Bosnia-Herzegovina. This included NATO's first-ever offensive strike on six Serbian jets that had violated the no-fly zone and bombed a Bosnian factory. Four were shot down.

The willingness of leadership to accept risk and "make things better" was apparent in every one of my subsequent deployments. It was expected that, as an airman, I would use my wits to overcome challenges and innovate in order to improve operations.

DEEPER INSIGHT

A leader who appreciates innovation and actively solicits input from the front lines will unleash creative energy, ideas, and change. However, this will occur only if both the leader and the organizational culture promote and support new ideas.

Taking a systems approach, innovation is "a large number of individuals working together in different units on different aspects of the very general problem of implementing a new idea" (Amabile, 1996).

Thus, innovation is not a top-down process. It is an organic and participative process and requires the diverse expertise and cooperation of several different functions. In addition, research shows that innovation occurs in organizations that exhibit four fundamental factors: leadership support, cultural support, process and administrative support, and open communication.

Professor Jeff DeGraff (2007) of the University of Michigan suggests that most innovation occurs at the edges of the organization. This is because the further you are away from the center, the less hold standard operating procedures (SOPs) have less hold over the outlying units. SOPs, while essential for sustaining organizational stability, are not conducive to the introduction of new ideas and variation.

Empirical research demonstrates a significant relationship between top leadership support of innovation and its actual occurrence within the organization (Chang & Lee, 2007; Jaskyte, 2004). Innovation is more likely to take place when it is accepted as a basic organizational value. Leaders can support innovative behavior by communicating its importance and demonstrating commitment through policies, procedures, and resource allocation.

That said, it's important to remember that there will always be tension between the ongoing operations of an organization and the need to innovate. On the one hand, your current operations are ostensibly producing results. Why change what's working? On the other hand, innovation is needed to create new processes, products, and services in order to adapt to changing conditions.

From this perspective, you must risk changing what's working and innovate so the organization continues to thrive.

RECAP

1. Innovation arises from a culture that supports it.

2. The "front lines" of an organization can be the source of natural innovation.

3. An innovative culture requires leadership support.

4. Innovation must be backed by policies, procedures, and allocation of resources.

5. Innovation requires the willingness to risk making changes, even when they don't seem necessary.

SELF-COACHING QUESTIONS

1. How enthusiastically does your organizational culture accept and support innovation?

2. What is your attitude toward and approach to innovation?

3. How do your people respond when it comes to the need to innovate? How open is your team to seeking creative, new methods and solutions?

4. How do you facilitate the required interaction and communication needed for innovation to occur?

INSIGHT #13

"We few, we happy few, we band of brothers"
The Absolute Importance of Strong, Functioning Relationships

"We few, we happy few, we band of brothers;
for he today that sheds his blood with me;
Shall be my brother."
—*William Shakespeare,* Henry V, *Act 4, Scene 3, Lines 62-64*

THE BOND THAT WARRIORS FORM in combat has been immortalized by many throughout the centuries, including Shakespeare in his famous soliloquy in *Henry V.* These relationships foster unit cohesion, fighting spirit, and military performance. Once experienced, the depth of these relationships has an enduring quality not often seen in other professions.

If we examine our definition of leadership more closely, we see two aspects that are integral to this discussion. The first is the notion of performance. A leader must produce results. The second is the need for leaders to work through others to achieve those results. Herein lies the importance of relationships: a leader must have strong-functioning relationships to achieve great results.

Shakespeare's King Henry is an excellent example of someone whose strong relationships were a springboard to extraordinary results. He was supported in his expedition to France by his brothers, Gloucester and Bedford; his uncle, Exeter; his cousin, York; and the earls of Salisbury, Westmoreland, and Warwick. Both they and his army stuck with him even though they were outnumbered by as many as ten to one by heavily armored French knights and accompanying forces. Henry's army ended up defeating the flower of the French aristocracy in the mud of Agincourt.

Perhaps you have been part of a team where mutual trust, understanding, and support led to outstanding performance. If so, you know the power of strong relationships.

DEEPER INSIGHT

Robert R. Blake and Jane Mouton (1964) first articulated the importance of leader-follower relationships with their managerial grid model. The managerial grid identified five leadership styles based on a manager's bias toward concern for production or concern for people. Ideally, a leader could select the particular style that suited the situation at hand and then vary the focus on results or relationships as required.

The leader-member exchange (LMX) theory of leadership goes beyond the managerial grid by focusing on the two-way relationship between supervisors and subordinates. LMX puts relationships at the center of leadership.

LMX focuses on increasing organizational success by creating positive relations between you and your subordinates. This theory assumes that leaders develop a professional relationship with each of their subordinates and that the quality of these relationships influences subordinates' responsibilities, decisions, access to resources, and performance.

LMX posits that leaders will naturally form two main groups of subordinates: an in-group and an out-group. Because the leader relates better to those in the in-group, they are given greater responsibilities, more latitude, more rewards, and more attention. They become the leader's "trusted lieutenants."

In contrast, out-group members get less attention, receive fewer rewards, and are managed in accordance with formal rules and policies. Out-group members often exhibit alienation, apathy, hostility, and low performance.

In LMX theory, the idea is for leaders to develop high-quality relationships with as many subordinates as possible. The objective is for the leader to expand her relationships with subordinates as widely as possible to include everyone, not just the in-group.

LMX theory suggests that leaders should (1) form productive, supportive relationships with all subordinates, (2) offer subordinates opportunities for new roles and responsibilities, and (3) build high-quality relationships with all subordinates.

LMX studies over the years have clearly demonstrated that the better the relationship between leader and follower, the higher the productivity, job satisfaction, motivation, and citizenship behavior of the follower. In addition, extensive research on LMX has shown a number of benefits to the organization, including:

- Less employee turnover
- More positive performance evaluations
- Higher frequency of promotions
- Greater organizational commitment from both managers and employees
- More desirable work assignments for subordinates
- Better employee job attitudes
- More attention and support from the leader
- Greater employee participation
- Faster career progress

What does it take to create the type of relationships that produce these benefits? LMX theory outlines a three-step process a leader should undertake:

- **Role taking:** When a new employee joins your organization, you assess her talent and abilities and offer her opportunities to demonstrate her skills.

- **Role making:** This is the informal back-and-forth between you and the new team member as you both "figure each other out." It is where trust develops. If the member happens to be like you in personality, background, and work ethic, the relationship and the member are more likely to succeed. If a member doesn't quite click with you or for some reason betrays your trust and confidence, she will most likely be relegated to the out-group.

- **Routinization:** This phase is where the relationship has been fully established to the point of routine. A person who finds herself in the in-group will work hard to stay in your good graces. If that team member is in the out-group, she will probably dislike or distrust you.

LMX is one of the most studied and validated theories in the leadership literature, but theory and practice are two separate things. You have to put LMX in practice in order to see the benefits. Not only that, as a leader, you are the one most responsible for creating in-groups and out-groups.

If your objective is to make your in-group as large as possible and thus increase the engagement and performance of your entire team, it is incumbent on you to take steps to assess your out-group and decrease its size. This requires you to take personal responsibility and approach the task with a large dose of humility.

Here is a process and some accompanying questions you can use to move the members of your out-group to your in-group:

- Analyze your entire team.
  ‣ Who are your favorites? Whom do you relate to best? Who are your top performers?
  ‣ Who are your least favorites? Whom do you dislike? Who are your poor performers?
- Identify the individuals in your out-group by name.
- Analyze the reasons these people are in the out-group.
  ‣ How are they unlike you?
  ‣ What did they do to cause you to relegate them to the out-group?
- Commit to rebuilding relationships with the out-group.
- Open communication channels with team members in the out-group, and start paying attention to their needs and aspirations.
  ‣ Can you describe their personalities?
  ‣ Where do they excel?
  ‣ What do they do in their off time?
  ‣ How are they similar to you?
  ‣ What are their aspirations?
- Understand their motivational drivers, development needs, and career interests.
  ‣ What motivates them?
  ‣ What can you do to help them grow their skills?
  ‣ How can you help them advance?
- Identify and provide opportunities to align their career goals with organizational goals.
- Provide training, mentoring, coaching, and other developmental opportunities.
- Score yourself on the quality of these relationships. If the scores continue to decrease or stay the same, reassess your approach and adjust accordingly.

★ ★ ★

The managerial grid model and LMX theory place relationships at the center of the leadership process. Both offer insights you can use to improve your ability to form trusting and mutually supportive relationships that will reduce the internal conflict that detracts from organizational performance and positive results.

RECAP

1. Leadership is a people business, and you ignore the quality of your professional relationships at your own peril.

2. Models like the managerial grid and LMX provide well-researched approaches for leaders to use to create and sustain strong relationships.

3. LMX reinforces the all-important role the leader plays in building inclusive teams.

4. It is up to leaders to initiate the process of rebuilding relationships that have gotten off to a bad start or are stagnated.

SELF-COACHING QUESTIONS

1. How big is your out-group?

2. Who is in your out-group, and why are they there?

3. How do you interact differently with the members of your in-group and out-group?

4. What are the advantages and disadvantages to you of having an in-group and an out-group?

5. How do the groups perceive each other?

6. What is the effect of such groups on the work environment and relationships within your organization?

7. What are the organizational consequences of poor relationships?

8. What can you do to build or rebuild relationships with your people?

INSIGHT #14

Handling the Politics of Leadership
Successfully Navigate Your Political Force Field

"One of the penalties for refusing to participate in politics is that
you end up being governed by your inferiors."
—*Plato*, Republic, *1:137*

ANY TIME A GROUP of smart, ambitious, type-A, competitive,
achievement-oriented people gets together, there will be conflict
of various kinds. Paraphrasing von Clausewitz (1832), the Prussian general and author of the military literary masterpiece *On
War*, leadership is the continuation of politics by other means.

As a leader, you will experience disagreements, deals gone sour,
questionable ethics, undermining, backbiting, and all of the nasty
things that arise when the stakes are high, resources are scarce,
power is to be gained or lost, and reputations are on the line.
Nonetheless, heroic leaders must be able to navigate through the
turbulence to achieve the results for which they are accountable
and to take care of the people they lead.

This is because when ambition, ego, and moral shortcomings are combined with power and control, a volatile mixture is created; and the higher you go, the more potentially explosive it becomes. It's like going from minor league ball to the big leagues: you have to know how to handle a major-league curveball to be successful.

You're going to have to deal with unsavory situations and people. Not everyone is wholesome in this world, and there are more than a few who will never understand the meaning of the word *integrity*.

I learned about the political force field and how to navigate it through the school of hard knocks. It was rougher for me than it needed to be because early in my career, I was quite certain that my take on things was the correct one. So if others didn't agree or had a different opinion, I had a tendency to dismiss them—not good if the people you dismiss are either your bosses or people you need to help you succeed. I also was overly trusting of people.

For me, being overly trusting was hardest to change because I had been fortunate in my youth and young adulthood to have been brought up in an environment in which I could trust people: family, friends, and coworkers. Over time, I realized that the trust I had known was indeed a precious gift.

I had to learn to be much more cautious and circumspect in my dealings with people, a sad reality to be sure, but a necessary skill to master in life.

DEEPER INSIGHT

So, how does a leader successfully navigate the political landscape?

The ideal policy would be to act with integrity and assume that those around you will do the same. Since the real world falls short of the ideal, you must resort to other methods to secure your flanks and your success.

The first key is to know what you believe in and remain grounded in your values. You're playing in the arena of high-level professional politics whether you like it or not. My advice is to always play your game with integrity. It is neither necessary nor advisable in the long run to sacrifice your values.

The second key is to realize that you are not perfect and in some way are contributing to the political force field. This realization should come with a big dose of humility. Take the medicine; it'll be good for you. Then, refer to the first key.

The third key is to always remain aware of the current status of your political environment. This is actually the toughest task and takes some effort to accomplish, but this skill is absolutely critical if you want to play in the big leagues and continue to do what you are called on to do as a leader.

Here is a process you can use to map out your political force field, remain aware of your status within it, and take action to navigate it with confidence.

- Identify the key actors who make up the political situation in which you find yourself. The first step is to list all the people who control, influence, or otherwise affect your ability to produce results and achieve your goals. On this list:
  - ▸ Include their titles and a brief description of the role they play in the system.
  - ▸ Indicate how much power they have to affect the outcome you seek (no power, some power, a lot of power, total control).
  - ▸ Identify the quality of your relationships with these people (terrible, standoffish, neutral, solid, excellent).
  - ▸ Indicate where you think they stand on your role, issue, project, or goal (no support, neutral, strong support).
  - ▸ Identify how they can help you (very little, some, a lot).

‣ Include your assessment of their willingness to help you (not at all, somewhat, very willing).

• Understand the professional aspirations and psychological dynamics of these influencers. When it comes right down to it, people are motivated by "What's in it for me?" Therefore, it behooves you to understand where those in your political force field are coming from. This knowledge will help you determine what is motivating them to behave and act the way they do. The objective is to build an informal psychological and behavioral "dossier" on those in your force field. Toward this end, answer these questions:

‣ What were their backgrounds in terms of upbringing and education?

‣ What career track did they follow?

‣ Who are their mentors?

‣ How do they behave on a day-to-day basis?

‣ How do they act under stress?

‣ How do they treat their friends?

‣ How do they treat their enemies?

‣ How do they treat their subordinates?

‣ What are their professional goals?

‣ What is most important to them professionally?

‣ What is most important to them personally?

‣ What are their personal interests?

‣ What do you know about their family relationships?

‣ Where do they spend most of their time?

‣ What issues are in the forefront of their minds?

‣ What are their needs for inclusion and significance?

- ▸ What are their needs for control and competence?
- ▸ What are their needs for openness and likability?
- ▸ What is their risk tolerance?
- ▸ How do they make decisions?
- ▸ What talents, skills, gifts, and strengths do they have?
- ▸ What makes them angry, irritated, or frustrated?
- ▸ Who influences them?

- The next step is to assess how you can manage the relationships with those in your political force field—at best, nurturing and improving them and, at worst, merely containing them. To do this, ask yourself these questions:
  - ▸ How do these people rate your relationships?
  - ▸ How do I rate these relationships?
  - ▸ Are these ratings close or far apart?
  - ▸ How often do I interact with these people?
  - ▸ Do I involve them in areas of mutual concern?
  - ▸ Do I ask them for advice?
  - ▸ Do I listen to and acknowledge any advice I might receive?
  - ▸ How well do I understand their commitments, aspirations, goals, values, challenges, pet peeves, and hot buttons?
  - ▸ Do I ask them how I can help them achieve their commitments, aspirations, and goals?
  - ▸ Do they tell me that they can trust me to keep my word and follow through?
  - ▸ Would they say that I have integrity?
  - ▸ Do I acknowledge their contributions, support, and successes?

- ▸ If my communication with them is suboptimal, do I ask how I can improve?

- ▸ Do I apologize for mistakes I have made in working with them?

- ▸ Do I state clearly what I expect and whether they are meeting my expectations?

- ▸ Do they know my commitments, aspirations, goals, values, challenges, pet peeves, and hot buttons?

- ▸ Have I told them how they bring value to me?

- ▸ Do I harbor resentment, jealousy, envy, anger, or animosity toward them?

- ▸ Do I focus on their talents, skills, gifts, and strengths rather than their failings and shortcomings?

- ▸ Do they trust me enough to share sensitive information?

- ▸ Do they speak positively about me and my work contributions?

- ▸ Do they support me, even if it involves professional risk?

- Given all that you know about the people in your force field, including their impact on you, their issues, how they feel about you, and other information, the next step is to allocate your time to (1) help those who are most important to you, (2) convert those who can help you and therefore begin to help them as well, and (3) manage the relationships with those whom you are unable to realistically influence or relate to professionally in order to minimize their negative impact on you.

- The final step is to regularly review the status of your force field. There are two types of reviews. The first is the day-to-day mental updates you will do after interacting with these people or hearing about their words or actions. The second type of review is an extended update of your map, where you set aside time to think more deeply about what is going on, what has changed, and what is working or not working. Then you formulate a hypothesis about how your actions or the actions of others will affect the force field.

When you complete this process, you should have an excellent idea of what your political force field looks like and what it will take to move within it effectively.

★ ★ ★

If you were reading closely, you'll understand that your ability to move freely depends on the quality of your relationships with those in your force field. Thus, creating well-functioning relationships—especially with those with the most influence and impact—is critical to your ability to lead effectively.

RECAP

1. At all levels of leadership, but especially the higher levels, leadership interactions become more and more political.

2. In order to survive and prosper, leaders must be able to navigate within the political force field that exists around them.

3. The most important thing to remember is to always act with integrity.

4. Navigating your political force field requires that you know how and why it fluctuates and the effect these fluctuations have on you.

5. You can use a five-step process to identify the actors in your force field, understand and interpret their behavior, learn how you can help them and they you, and make adjustments as required.

SELF-COACHING QUESTIONS

1. How have "politics" affected your ability to lead?

2. How adept are you at the political game?

3. Do you act with integrity despite the political force field that exists around you? If not, what is keeping you from doing so?

4. What can you do to improve your understanding of your political force field and your ability to function effectively within it?

INSIGHT #15

Appreciate Your Friends, Allies, and Coalitions
Strengthening Your Power Base

LOOK BACK IN US HISTORY, and you'll see that in practically every war we've fought—save for the Civil War—we've had allies. In fact, you can make a good case that if it weren't for the French sending over their fleet and an army during the Revolutionary War, we'd still be part of the British empire.

Every professional military education course I attended in the Air Force always had a module dedicated to the challenges inherent in going to war alongside allies. The lesson that was drilled into us was this: America doesn't go to war alone; we always have allies. But allies bring with them their own sets of circumstances, priorities, and ideas, so it's never a clean situation.

That's doubtlessly a reason the military staff colleges and war colleges put such an emphasis on studying the challenge of fighting in partnership with allies: to help prepare students for what they would face in the event of a war.

The upshot of all this is that you'll rarely be able to go it alone as a leader. There will always be someone outside your span of control whose help you need to succeed. Also, there will always be others on your side who will seek to check your influence, try to enhance theirs, and even undermine your standing if that serves their interests (despite their role as allies).

At the organizational level, building formal strategic alliances and strong supplier relationships become the ways you need to achieve organizational goals. In military terms, think NATO. Or you might build a coalition of unlikely bedfellows to take on a particularly thorny regulatory or marketing issue; in this case, think the War on Terror's "coalition of the willing."

Similarly, from a professional standpoint, you will have allies, form coalitions, and have trusted friends whom you will need to help you achieve all that your role as a leader demands of you. In short, for better or for worse (one hopes for better), this is your power base; it behooves you to take care of it, build it, refine it, and continually strengthen it.

DEEPER INSIGHT

Your power base provides the energy for your political force field. The reality of leadership is that you are moving among people with power and influence. Some you can count as your friends, some as allies, others as neutral, and still others as part of a temporary coalition; and yes, there probably will be a few enemies or at least people who disagree with your point of view.

According to Harvard professor John Kotter, "...when a high degree of interdependence exists in the workplace, unilateral action is rarely possible. For all decisions of any significance, many people will be in a position to retard, block, or sabotage action because they have some power over the situation" (Kotter, 1985).

The other reality is that your relationships are always changing, shifting, and developing. This has an impact on your ability to operate in politically complex situations. Ultimately, you want to have a strong enough power base to be able to deal with this complexity and thus improve your ability to create the best environment in which to exercise your influence and get things done.

Your power base comprises your friends, allies, and coalition partners, each of whom is characterized by a different level of trust and commitment. You will be most able to trust and count on your friends. Your allies are those with whom you have some things in common and have built at least an acceptable level of trust based on experiences you've shared over time. With some allies, you may have established formal agreements that bind you to each other. Coalition partners are those who have agreed to work with you for a short period of time to achieve a common goal.

The idea is to continually build and strengthen the relationships with your friends, allies, and coalition partners as well as to establish new relationships. Work to create authentic, trusting relationships with the people who most affect your area of responsibility. Although quality is paramount, quantity also matters. As the Soviets used to say about the size of their military forces during the Cold War, "quantity has a quality all its own."

According to Raven and Kruglanski (1970) and Hersey and Goldsmith (1980), your power is derived from seven discrete bases:

- Coercive power, based on fear of consequences
- Legitimate power, based on position
- Expert power, based on your skill or knowledge
- Reward power, based on your ability to provide rewards
- Referent power, based on personal attributes
- Informational power, based on access to information
- Connection power, based on links with important people

In dealing with other leaders, it is a given that each of you will have some degree of coercive, legitimate, expert, and reward power. These elements of power operate within generally well-known boundaries, so there is not a lot of day-to-day room to maneuver. However, over time you might add to your education, move up in the organization, or have additional power conferred on you through organizational realignments.

The biggest opportunities to strengthen your professional power base come from increasing your referent, informational, and connection power. These three bases of power are much more relationship-oriented and are where you can see the biggest impact on your power base.

Increasing your referent power: Referent power is based on how well people relate to you. It's founded on your innate personality, emotional intelligence, and interpersonal skills. It depends on your negotiation and listening skills, your leadership presence, your willingness to empower your subordinates, and how generous you are with your expertise. Improve your referent power by strengthening any of these elements.

Increasing your informational power: The essence of increasing informational power is gaining, maintaining, and expanding your access to information so that you know in depth what's going on in the organization and why. In the military, it's called "information superiority." The idea is to have intimate knowledge of your political force field and what's going on that is important to the organization.

Gaining information superiority allows you to make faster, better, and smarter decisions—an obvious advantage for a leader. Again, the quality of your relationships is critical to your ability to stay informed and learn new information. In addition, it's important to have relationships with people who have access to vital information and to tap into resources that can supply you with the critical information you need.

Increasing your connection power: The rise of social networks is a sterling example of how being connected can work for you. Networking, in the sense of growing mutually supportive relationships, is really the heart of increasing your connection power. As you network and build relationships, make a point to connect with powerful people who score high in their reward, expert, referent, informational, and connection power. By connecting with powerful people, you have the opportunity to benefit from their power by proxy and increase your own.

★ ★ ★

In sum, a strong power base that comprises friends, allies, and coalition partners increases your ability to get things done as a leader.

RECAP

1. Your power base provides the energy of your political force field.

2. Having a strong power base is vital to your ability to lead and thus get things done.

3. Your power base is made up of your friends, allies, and coalition partners. Each of these is characterized by a different level of trust and commitment.

4. Acknowledge the power dynamics associated with your power base and political force field, and work to build authentic, trusting relationships.

5. Of the seven discrete bases of leadership power, referent power, informational power, and connection power are the most expandable and therefore most worth the investment of your time and energy.

SELF-COACHING QUESTIONS

1. Who are your friends, allies, and coalition partners?

2. How would you characterize the quality of your relationships with them?

3. How large is your power base in terms of people, groups, and resources?

4. What can you do to improve the quality and size of your power base?

5. What can you do to increase your referent power?

6. What can you do to increase your informational power?

7. What can you do to increase your connection power?

INSIGHT #16

Getting What You Need
*Using Your Power Base for Influence
and Leverage to Get Things Done*

CONTRARY TO POPULAR BELIEF, the higher up the leadership chain you go, the harder it is to get things done.

At these levels, the stakes are also higher and the consequences more far-reaching than at the beginning of your journey. Also, ambitions and egos are larger, making your ability to deal with people very critical. Finally, increased leadership responsibility does not necessarily mean more control over desired outcomes. In fact, many times it means you have *less* control due to the size and type of organization, the politics in play, the resources required, and the resistance you face.

It is at this point that your ability to influence others and use leverage comes into play. Influence is your ability to persuade others to your way of thinking and gain their support for an idea, a particular course of action, or resources. Leverage is more about using your position to your best advantage in order to gain that support.

Let me give you an example. As the designated city manager at an Air Force base of twenty-three thousand people, I had twelve hundred people working for me directly. They were responsible for logistics, human resources, parks and recreation, transportation, policing, and contracting. However, I did *not* have under my direct control the other resources I needed to do my job effectively, such as public works, emergency and fire response, and sanitation. Finally, the budget I needed to run the operation effectively was continually under pressure and, in fact, faced constant cuts.

What I quickly learned was that any lasting success we might have hinged in part on my ability to influence my counterparts who *did* control those other areas. I needed to create positive leverage with them, while attempting to lobby for resources in the face of additional cuts.

I can tell you that I invested a lot of time in using my influence and creating leverage. It was not an easy or straightforward process. In fact, it became somewhat of a joke with my staff that to get anything done—no matter how big or small—required "the colonel" (me) to enter into high-level talks with my peers.

DEEPER INSIGHT

Your influence is a key determinant of how well you are able to navigate your political force field and achieve the outcomes you seek for your organization. According to psychologist Robert Cialdini (2007), influence arises from six universal principles:

- **Reciprocity:** If someone helps us, does us a favor, or treats us well, we feel obligated to return the kindness because we are uncomfortable with feeling indebted. I found reciprocity to be a way of life whenever I was deployed overseas. It was all about doing favors for and receiving favors from others in order to get anything done. I always seemed to have a "master scrounger" who was able to get just about anything we needed. This person relied on his influence in order to make trades and call in favors when necessary.

- **Commitment (and Consistency):** Once we've said yes to someone or agreed to a task, we're much more inclined to follow through. The idea here is to get a commitment, no matter how small, from the people you need on your side to move a project forward or accomplish other goals.

- **Social Proof:** If other people are doing something, then we are more likely to agree to do it, too. We like to know that others have pursued a particular course of action, idea, or decision. Social proof influences us most when we are uncertain, because we're looking for cues from those around us to confirm that what we want to do is prudent or worthwhile. For example, if you see others working late on a project, you might be more willing to do the same.

- **Liking:** If you like someone, you're more apt to be influenced by that person. You might like someone because you can relate to her, she makes you feel good, or because you trust her. As a leader, the more likable you are, the greater your influence over others will be.

- **Authority:** Someone in a position of authority naturally elicits a sense of obligation in others. People in authority have a certain credibility that can persuade us to accept what they say. For example, think of doctors or people in uniform. Their positions and what they do cause us to assume they know what they're talking about.

- **Scarcity:** When availability is limited or we might lose the opportunity to do or obtain something, the more attractive what we want becomes. Thus, scarcity can be leveraged to increase influence. For example, because the promise of a promotion or a meeting with the busy president of a potential client company has the quality of scarcity, your boss or the company president can use this scarcity to increase his influence over you.

Influence, as an element of power, is meant to be used. For each of the six principles above, here are suggestions for how to make it work for you.

- To use **reciprocity**, first think about what you want from the other person. Then, identify what you can give to him in return. Think about how you can "create a debt" in his mind.

- For **commitment**, secure someone's agreement early on either verbally or in writing. If you can get a *yes* on your entire idea, all the better, but even a small, incremental *yes* can secure commitment. For example, if you are pitching a product or service, give people a demo, sample, or trial run to invest them in the product or service and help ensure their full commitment later.

- **Social proof** can be achieved from numbers of sales or users, testimonials, citations in social media, customer case studies, or word-of-mouth referrals. The whole idea of social proof is to provide evidence from others that your idea, product, or service is worthwhile.

- Being **likable** means being able to relate to people in a way that makes them feel good and inspires trust. Two ways to develop your likability are to increase your emotional intelligence, or EQ (the ability to express and control our own emotions and to understand, interpret, and respond to the emotions of others), and your listening skills. Remember that people appreciate those who sincerely appreciate them.

- If you stay on top of your political force field, you'll have an excellent understanding of your **authority-based** influence. You communicate your authority and exert your influence through your job title, style, credentials, offices, and command of the language.

- Creating **scarcity** in an organization can be achieved by how resources are applied or not applied. Also, a sense of urgency can create scarcity by highlighting the consequences of not acting.

★ ★ ★

Two final points: First, make sure you use your influence in an ethical manner. It only takes one misstep for you to lose it. Second, influence is a perishable asset. You have to work at developing, sustaining, and growing it. Staying plugged into and aware of your political force field will help you do that.

RECAP

1. Influence is your ability to affect events and outcomes without necessarily being in control of them.

2. Influence is part and parcel of your political force field.

3. According to Dr. Robert Cialdini, there are six elements of influence: reciprocity, commitment, authority, likability, social proof, and scarcity.

4. Each of these elements can be used singly or in combination to exert influence.

5. Use your influence ethically, and remember that it is a perishable commodity.

SELF-COACHING QUESTIONS

1. How do I rate my overall influence (high, average, low)?
2. How do I rate my influencing strengths for each of the six elements?
3. Which element(s) do I need to work on most to increase my influence?
4. What am I doing to increase my ability to influence others?
5. In what areas of my professional life should I be influential?
6. What is my game plan to bolster my influence?

INSIGHT #17

"To End a War"
Negotiating Your Way to Success

THE LATE AMBASSADOR RICHARD HOLBROOKE described his part in the Dayton Accords that brought an end to hostilities in the Balkans in his book, *To End a War*. During three weeks of intense and trying negotiations, Holbrooke used all his considerable expertise and presence to progressively move the parties to a signed peace agreement. He was later awarded the Nobel Peace Prize for his efforts.

Achievements like this don't happen by accident. In Holbrooke's case, he had spent his career in diplomatic missions that demanded highly refined skills in sensitive negotiations.

DEEPER INSIGHT
Given the inherently political nature of leadership, being able to negotiate successfully is an essential competency for a leader. Your negotiation skills have a direct effect on your ability to gain agreement for ideas and courses of action, as well as to acquire support for your position.

Because negotiation skills are so important in your position, I recommend taking a course or other in-depth instruction and practice. That said, there are a few basic principles to keep in mind.

Integrative or interest-based bargaining: Do you want to hard bargain in a win-lose fashion, or do you want to negotiate in a way that expands value for all parties? The latter approach is often called integrative or interest-based negotiation. Most experts now recommend this approach as a way to ensure positive outcomes for all parties. Unlike traditional negotiations that assume there is only a fixed amount of value, interest-based negotiation seeks to expand the pie. This method builds on underlying shared interests to arrive at a mutually satisfying agreement between parties.

Best Alternative to a Negotiated Agreement (BATNA): BATNA is your course of action in the absence of a deal if the negotiation does not succeed. Knowing your BATNA means deciding what you will do or what will happen if you fail to reach agreement in the negotiation.

Reservation or the walk-away price: This is the least favorable point at which you will accept a deal. If you are a seller, the walk-away price is as low as you will go on price.

Zone of Potential Agreement (ZOPA): ZOPA pertains to the parameters that satisfy both parties. For example, if an IT contractor provides a $250,000 quote to perform a project, but you are willing to pay only $200,000, then you have no ZOPA. However, you may be willing to offer the contractor follow-up work for $50,000 if he is successful with the initial project. In this case, you may have a ZOPA because each party has a basis from which to meet its basic requirements.

Assertiveness: Being assertive does not mean being aggressive, overly emotional, or abrasive. However, you cannot negotiate unless you are willing to challenge the opposing position. It means being rational, challenging everything, and believing that everything is negotiable. Being assertive means asking for what you want and taking care of your own interests while maintaining respect for the interests of others.

Listening well: Good negotiators know how to ask questions and listen. The idea is to elicit more information from the other party that will help in the negotiation process. One technique to do this is the ten-second strategy. Quite simply, be quiet for ten seconds, and wait for the other party to break the silence.

★ ★ ★

The ability to negotiate effectively is vital to your success. A lack of solid negotiating skills can lead to reduced effectiveness on your part and increased cost to the organization. Leaders who know how to negotiate often get what they want in a way that facilitates positive relationships and cooperation when it comes time to negotiate again. There are few leadership challenges that can't be helped by an adept negotiator.

RECAP

1. Knowing how to negotiate effectively is a key leadership skill.
2. Negotiation experts recommend interest-based negotiation in which all parties seek to expand mutual value as an outcome of the negotiation.
3. Know your BATNA, reservation price, and ZOPA before you negotiate.
4. Do your homework, and prepare well for the negotiation meeting.

5. Understand what assertiveness means and practice assertive, not aggressive, behavior.

6. Take a course, get private instruction, or read about negotiating to sharpen your negotiating skills.

SELF-COACHING QUESTIONS

1. How successful at negotiations have I been in my career?

2. How do I assess my ability to negotiate (beginner, novice, competent, expert)?

3. How well do I prepare for important negotiations, including those with my peers?

4. How can I improve my negotiating skills?

INSIGHT #18

Peacetime and Wartime Decision Making
Having the Courage to Make Decisions That Count

IF ACHIEVING QUALITY RESULTS is the ultimate purpose of leadership, then being able to make good decisions is a fundamental prerequisite for getting those results.

Whenever I mentored my young officers, I always pointed out to them that their ability to make good decisions was their "bread and butter" as leaders, because, when push came to shove, they would be held accountable for the performance of the mission, and the quality of the decisions they made would have a direct impact on the outcome.

Every day, leaders everywhere make decisions large and small that affect the well-being and future of the organizations they serve. It takes real skill to make good decisions.

Leaders must be able to make decisions that reliably chart a course to the future, ideally using a deliberate process. This is similar to military peacetime decision making, when there is ostensibly more time to analyze decisions that will affect the ability of the armed forces to prevail in future conflicts. Those who work in the Pentagon might disagree, however, given the baffling way that bureaucratic fires spring up.

Leaders must also be able to respond well to crises and pressure, when making good "gut" decisions really counts. In these types of emergency situations, you may not have time to think, analyze, or investigate all the risks. Employing your intuition and experience, you must make decisions quickly based on the information at hand.

For example, I was once called on to orchestrate the recovery of two five-hundred-pound bombs and two one-thousand-pound fuel tanks that had been jettisoned from an F-16 fighter aircraft during an in-flight emergency. This situation had taken place in a munitions storage area smack dab in the middle of an Air Force base surrounded by densely populated residential neighborhoods.

I was getting advice from all directions at a rapid-fire rate. Calls were coming in from national media, the governor's office, and headquarters. We had coordinated with the state highway patrol to shut down the interstate, and traffic was backing up for miles. We had received numerous reports from off-base residents about sightings of objects that looked like bombs. Plus, it was getting dark.

At that moment, the most important decision I had to make was where to send the explosive ordinance search teams. As I listened to everyone's input, the information that made the most sense came from two seasoned fighter pilots who were sitting a couple of chairs down from me. They said that there was no way that the second bomb could have drifted two miles from where the first one landed. It was a matter of physics. So I decided to constrain the search to the base.

It turns out I made the right decision. We found both tanks and the second bomb within a two-hundred-meter radius of each other just before night fell.

DEEPER INSIGHT

In both peacetime and wartime situations, courage is required to step up and make decisions that count—decisions that move the organization forward in the most prudent and effective way possible. In most cases, no decision will be absolutely ideal, nor will everyone be pleased. There will be times when the outcome is not exactly as anticipated or a decision must be modified.

Nonetheless, your job as a leader is to make good decisions no matter how much pressure you feel. A rational decision-making process will help ensure that you make the best decision possible. It will also help you recognize the nuances of your decision and balance the conflicts and emotions that may surround it.

Here are some tactics that can help when you find yourself faced with tough decisions:

- **Take charge of the decision:** There is a time to delegate decisions, but if this is a tough one, get engaged. Your chances of success increase when you have "skin in the game."

- **Seek to understand:** You will have a tendency to revert to your frame of reference for the decision, especially under pressure. It will also be tempting to pay attention to only the most sensational aspects of the situation. Instead, take some time to reflect on core issues. Work to appreciate other perspectives. Uncover the underlying "why" of what needs fixing. In so doing, you will arrive at a broader understanding of the decision and different avenues for solving the problem.

- **Establish clear direction:** Set an objective that everyone involved can clearly identify with. This establishes the rationale for action and provides all-important focus for the team.

- **Create and promote ideas that generate action:** This requires you to be open to other ideas without bias and to promote the best ideas within the context of your particular political force field. Your ultimate goal is to secure agreement for action.

- **Identify more than one option:** Options are a natural consequence of generating ideas and provide a means of comparing the merits of one course of action over another. Multiple options open you up to alternative perspectives.

- **Deal with resistance and barriers to action:** Just because you make a well-informed decision doesn't mean it will be accepted or carried out. Incorporate real and potential obstacles to your decision up front, and formulate solutions to overcome them. Explicitly address the "politics" of implementing the decision.

In the final analysis, you are responsible for making the tough calls. No one knew this better than General Dwight Eisenhower during the lead-up to D-Day. The scheduled day of the invasion and the date to which all Allied planning and preparation had been targeted was June 5, when the tides would be most favorable. It was also the day the Russians were to launch their offensive to the west into Germany.

But the Allies were also experiencing the worst storm over the English Channel in twenty years. The consequences of delay were enormous for the largest amphibious invasion in world history: four thousand warships, nearly ten thousand aircraft, and 160,000 invasion troops.

Eisenhower postponed the invasion for twenty-four hours in the hope that the weather would clear sufficiently to give the order to move the next day. When a visibly strained Eisenhower consulted with his staff that evening, forecasters projected a brief lessening of the storm on June 6. After a few moments of introspection, Eisenhower rose and said, "Well, we'll go."

The results of the invasion are now a matter of history as is Eisenhower's famous dispatch of its success. What is less well known is that Eisenhower had written another message in case the landing failed:

"Our landings in the Cherbourg-Havre area have failed to gain a satisfactory foothold, and I have withdrawn the troops. My decision to attack at this time and place was based on the best information available. The troops, the air and the Navy did all that bravery and devotion to duty could do. If any blame or fault attaches to the attempt, it is mine alone."

★ ★ ★

It takes courage to make tough decisions when the stakes are incredibly high. But leadership demands tough decisions, and these tactics for decision making are a good place to start.

RECAP

1. Making decisions—especially tough decisions—is a leader's stock-in-trade.

2. Leaders need courage to make tough decisions.

3. Tough decisions are usually fraught with conflict and emotion.

4. Having a rational decision-making process will help ensure that a leader makes balanced, comprehensive, well-analyzed, and well-informed decisions, even under pressure.

5. Leader engagement is a must on tough decisions.

6. Understanding other perspectives, generating ideas, crafting options, dealing with the "politics," and overcoming resistance are all part of making a tough decision.

SELF-COACHING QUESTIONS

1. What decisions have I made in the past that required courage?

2. What were the results?

3. What are some ways I can improve my ability to make tough decisions?

INSIGHT #19

"Life Is Tough, but It's Tougher if You're Stupid"
How to Work the Wicked Problems

JOHN WAYNE'S famous quote from *The Sands of Iwo Jima* serves as a catchphrase for what it takes to face down the inevitable challenges that will come your way. There are two general rules in play here:

- The higher you rise in your organization, the more difficult the problems become.

- You will be tempted to spend a lot of time on the simple problems and avoid the vexing ones. This is not wise.

"Wicked problems" are difficult or impossible to solve because of incomplete, contradictory, and changing requirements. In addition, the effort to solve one aspect of the problem may reveal or create other ones. Wicked problems arise from within the system; consequently, any attempt to solve them affects the system, often in unpredictable and surprising ways.

DEEPER INSIGHT

According to Horst Rittel and Melvin Webber (1973), wicked problems have the following characteristics:

- It is not possible to write a well-defined statement of the problem, as can be done with an ordinary problem.

- They have no point at which they are absolutely resolved. You can tell when you've reached a solution for an ordinary problem, but with a wicked one, the search for solutions never ends.

- Ordinary problems have solutions that can be objectively evaluated as right or wrong. Formulating a solution to a wicked problem is largely a matter of judgment.

- There is no immediate or ultimate test of a solution. With an ordinary problem, it is possible to determine right away if a solution is working. But solutions to wicked problems generate unexpected consequences over time, making it difficult to measure their effectiveness.

- Every solution to a wicked problem is a "one-shot" experiment. There is no opportunity to learn by trial and error. Every implemented solution has consequences that cannot be undone. In contrast, solutions to ordinary problems can easily be tried and abandoned.

- Wicked problems do not have an unlimited set of potential solutions or a well-prescribed set of options that may be incorporated into the plan. In contrast, ordinary problems have a number of possible solutions.

- Every wicked problem is essentially unique. It is without precedent; experience does not help you address it. An ordinary problem belongs to a class of similar problems that are all solved in similar ways.

- Every wicked problem can be considered to be a symptom of another problem. While an ordinary problem is self-contained, a wicked problem is intertwined with other problems.

- A wicked problem involves many stakeholders, all of whom have different ideas about what the problem really is and what caused it.

Examples of wicked problems include nearly any public policy issue or corporate strategy, such as post-invasion Iraq, the Israeli-Palestinian peace process, and climate change.

Wicked problems can also be characterized as "messes" endemic to complex systems of systems. According to Robert Horn (2007), a social mess is defined by the following characteristics:

- No unique or "correct" view of the problem
- Different views of the problem and contradictory solutions
- Most problems connected to other problems
- Data often uncertain or missing
- Multiple value conflicts
- Ideological, cultural, political, and economic constraints
- Often illogical or multi-valued thinking
- Numerous possible intervention points
- Consequences difficult to imagine
- Considerable uncertainty, ambiguity
- Great resistance to change
- Problem solver(s) out of contact with problem and potential solutions

Wicked problems force you to adopt another approach to problem solving. The work required is not solely intellectual; it is also a social and political task that requires all of your talent, skill, and experience to persevere until you establish a viable way forward. It also requires an open, experimental, interdisciplinary approach.

For example, the technique of dialogue mapping allows diverse stakeholders to build a shared understanding of the problem and create a joint commitment to its solution. Dialogue mapping uses a special method of structured facilitation to focus, clarify, and engage participants as they work on the problem.

George Day and Paul Schoemaker (2005) suggest a way of learning from the past and present as well as thinking about the future that can help identify wicked problems before they become major issues. In order to do this, they suggest asking the following questions:

To learn from the past

- Where are past blind spots?
- What is happening in those areas now?
- Is there an instructive analogy or case study that will shed light on the problem?
- Who among our competitors is acting ahead of everyone else?

To examine the present

- What environmental signals are we rationalizing away?
- What does scenario planning or future planning tell us about today's signals?
- What are the mavericks or social outliers saying?
- What are peripheral customers and competitors doing?

To envision the future

- What could really hurt us?
- How would we attack our own business?
- What technologies could change the game?
- Is there a worst-case scenario?

★ ★ ★

The key here is to move past your conventional problem-solving tendencies and adopt processes, methods, and techniques that are more suitable for dealing with wicked problems. Wicked problems are tough, but it's up to you to work through them.

RECAP

1. As a leader, you will be faced with wicked problems.
2. Wicked problems are not really solved per se, but rather dealt with.
3. Attacking wicked problems requires an alternative problem-solving approach.
4. Leaders can use dialogue mapping, scenario planning, and environmental scanning to tackle wicked problems and develop courses of action to deal with them.

SELF-COACHING QUESTIONS

1. What skills do I have that will help me deal with wicked problems?
2. What skills does my organization or team have?
3. What problems of this nature am I facing now?
4. How well is my current problem-solving approach working?
5. What can I do to improve my ability to tackle wicked problems?

INSIGHT #20

Attack in Any Direction
How to Deal with the Pressures of Leadership

"So they've got us surrounded, good! Now we can fire
in any direction; those bastards won't get away this time!"
—*Chesty Puller, USMC*

MARINE COLONEL CHESTY PULLER uttered this statement
during the battle at Chosin Reservoir in Korea where United
Nations forces found themselves surrounded and outnumbered
by Chinese troops in bitterly cold and arduous conditions. After
seventeen days of ferocious fighting, the United Nations army was
able to break out of the encirclement.

Seventeen Medals of Honor were bestowed for gallantry during
this battle, and the stories of the hardships, endurance, and leadership at Chosin are legendary. The Battle of Chosin Reservoir stands
as an example of what it means to drive on under duress.

When you lead others, there are going to be times when it seems
difficult to continue, when your personal reserves are depleted;
but nonetheless, your leadership will be required.

It may not be as life-imperiling as fighting a tenacious adversary at Chosin Reservoir, but it could be declining market share, an ethical scandal, an unanticipated emergency, or unrelenting pressure from above to achieve results. In any event, when storm clouds have gathered and you are in dark hours, you must continue to find a way to lead.

US Special Forces training is deliberately tough. It is designed to tax trainees to the maximum extent of their physical and mental capabilities—and then push beyond them. The idea is to select members who show the fortitude to perform even under the most difficult and trying conditions. Only a few make it, and those who do are asked to perform missions where difficulty, danger, and duress are ever present.

Of necessity, leadership under these circumstances must be resolute and decisive despite the physical, psychological, and intellectual resources demanded of you. Similarly, you must be able to draw on your inner reserves to drive on under duress and continue to provide the level of leadership required of you.

DEEPER INSIGHT

Ultimately, developing grace under pressure means learning how to act in concert with fear. It is fear that produces the pressure you feel. According to Fundamental Interpersonal Relations Orientation (FIRO) theory, fears arise from feelings of incompetence, insignificance, and unlikability. Fear can also result from threats to our well-being.

The first thing to realize about fear is that the reptilian part of our brains is hardwired to deal with it. The adage about fight, flight, or freeze is true. Once fear engages the brain, it, not your intellect, is in charge. As such, the ability of the cerebral cortex to dictate your actions through reasoning is diminished.

Second, although we all experience fear, each of us reacts to it differently—some better than others. Research conducted by a British officer named Lionel Wigram at the outset of World War II showed that soldiers under fire responded in three distinct ways: a few would panic; most would freeze; and a few stayed cool and performed valiantly. More recent research by survival psychologist John Leach (1994) with random groups of people during an emergency showed a similar pattern: 10 to 15 percent panicked; 65 to 80 percent froze; and 10 to 20 percent took positive action. What this means is that at least a part of our ability to perform under pressure is probably genetically determined.

What you are really after is the ability to perform well *despite* the fear you may be experiencing, in other words, to operate *in concert* with the fear. This is where elite special forces excel. In fact, the training they undergo develops, enhances, and strengthens this ability.

The same applies to leaders under pressure. If you practice under realistic conditions, you will react and perform better when similar events actually occur. Structured preparation strengthens skill circuits that kick in and work along with fear and pressure so that performance remains effective.

You can also work on your attitude toward pressure. According to Justin Menkes (2011), leaders who perform under stress exhibit realistic optimism, subservience to purpose, and the ability to find order in chaos. As realistic optimists, "they recognize the risks threatening their organization's survival—and their own failings— while remaining confident in their ability to have an impact." These leaders also commit themselves to a higher purpose and secure their team's commitment to it as well. By finding order in chaos, they are able to sort through the noise and focus on what really matters for the success of their organizations. So even though your brain is in emergency mode, the way you frame the situation in your mind can influence how you deal with it.

The real shift occurs when you are able to harness your pressure to help you perform. Everyone experiences it, but the difference between elite performers and amateurs is that the elite performers have learned how to channel their fears into action. They have learned to embrace their fear as a friend rather than as the enemy.

★ ★ ★

The more you welcome fear, the more you learn to work with it, and the more you prepare, the better able you will be to call on your intellect and skills to lead like a champion. Like Chesty Puller, you'll be able to fire at the enemy (the challenges you face) in any direction.

RECAP

1. Being a leader means that you will experience multifaceted and demanding pressures.

2. The underlying cause of pressure is fear.

3. It is impossible to overcome fear, but it is possible to deal with it productively.

4. When you experience fear, the control of your brain switches from rational thinking to an emotionally driven "flight, fight, or freeze" reaction.

5. Regular and realistic practice of pressure-inducing situations improves your ability to deal with fear.

6. Adopt an accepting attitude toward fear and pressure.

7. Realize that everyone experiences fear, but elite leaders harness it and the pressure that comes with it to their benefit.

SELF-COACHING QUESTIONS

1. On a ten-point scale, how do you rate your ability to deal with pressure?

2. What is your primary method of dealing with pressure?

3. What is your present attitude toward pressure?

4. How do you harness fear and pressure to your benefit?

5. What are some ways to improve your ability to deal with pressure and perform well?

INSIGHT #21

Avoiding Tunnel Vision
Open the Aperture to Gain Perspective

"We cannot solve our problems with the same level
of thinking that created them."
—*Albert Einstein*

WHEN THEY COME IN for a strafing or bombing run, fighter pilots use a sighting mechanism called a target aperture to ensure that the jet is lined up optimally. However, hard-won experience and training have taught them not to get overly fixated on that narrow aperture because too many pilots who did so have crashed. In fact, the term "target fixation" arose out of World War II fighter-pilot training to describe pilots who flew into targets during a strafing or bombing run.

For fighter pilots, opening the aperture means widening their field of view to take in more information about the overall aerial situation and maintaining situational awareness. This is one way to ensure the success of the mission and live to fly another day.

When your leadership aperture is too small, you can become so intently focused on a particular problem that you fail to see other challenges that may be hazardous to your organization. A good example was the focus on how to reduce the cost of producing buggy whips when motor cars were already starting to cruise the streets.

DEEPER INSIGHT

Being able to open your aperture is a critical skill, especially when you are under pressure or during a crisis when your options seem to disappear. Under such circumstances, when "something must be done," you may have the tendency to revert to "default" behavior and exhibit analytical and decision-making biases that are inappropriate for the current situation.

Expanding your view is also important because the higher up you go in the organization, the less willing your people will be to disagree with you. This means that you can get trapped into thinking that your ideas and solutions are the best ones. All of these factors can lead to bad decision making and negative consequences for the organization.

However, there are several things you can do to avoid this scenario, including systems thinking, scanning your environment, seeking out alternative views, and using case studies.

Systems thinking allows you to view the entire forest instead of getting stuck in the trees. Inherent in systems thinking is viewing problems in terms of how the parts relate to the whole. This holistic view keeps you from getting fixated on specific details at the expense of the bigger picture.

Environmental scanning is a structured way of painting a bigger picture of the system in which your organization operates. It consists of an analysis of internal and external assessments and of strengths, weaknesses, opportunities, and threats. You then use this analysis to evaluate strategic gaps in the context of the broader tapestry of the societal milieu, economic movements, legal frameworks, political constraints, and industry trends. In so doing, you become better positioned to align your strategic approach with the tactical initiatives that will produce success for the organization.

Seeking out alternative views means that you must cross-check your beliefs, opinions, and ideas against different viewpoints. This requires the courage to ask for input from others and the willingness to modify your stance if the circumstances dictate. Seeking alternative views can help prevent you from being too intellectually, psychologically, politically, or emotionally invested in an idea, thus closing yourself off to valuable input that improves your understanding of the particular challenge you face.

A good example of this is the way Lincoln populated his war cabinet with his political rivals. By doing so, he integrated alternative perspectives that allowed him to stay more closely attuned to the political system in which he was operating. This approach became a built-in mechanism to challenge and broaden his thinking about the momentous issues he faced.

Using case studies enables top-tier business schools to create a databank of analogous experiences to assist students with challenges that arise in leading an organization. However, the key to using case studies is to look not for *similarities* but rather for the *differences* between your situation and the relevant case. Toward this end, make sure you separate what is known about the situation from what is unclear, and beware of easy analogies when current circumstances differ from those of the cases. This will ensure that you don't become so overly preoccupied with similarities and solutions that are inadequate for the situation at hand.

★ ★ ★

Keeping your aperture open is a crucial skill for a leader. By employing systems thinking, continually scanning your environment, listening to other viewpoints, and using case studies, you stand a better chance of not losing your perspective and becoming "target fixated."

RECAP

1. "Target fixation" is as dangerous for a leader as it is for a fighter pilot.

2. Closing your mind to other ideas, becoming excessively focused on details, and being single-minded all contribute to loss of perspective.

3. To maintain perspective, you must "open your aperture."

4. Techniques to achieve this include systems thinking, environmental scanning, seeking alternative views, and using case studies.

SELF-COACHING QUESTIONS

1. How well do you maintain your perspective, especially under pressure?

2. How do you rate your ability to listen to viewpoints other than your own?

3. Are you able to think in terms of the entire system as well as details?

4. How well do you scan your environment?

5. What can you do to improve your ability to open your aperture?

INSIGHT #22

Trusted Advisers and Mentors
The Importance of High-Quality Advice

US PRESIDENTS SURROUND THEMSELVES with a cadre of trusted advisers who assist them with problems, decisions, and tough issues. Presidential advisers come in all types. You name the area, and the president probably has an adviser on it.

Having people you can trust to offer their expertise in honest and candid ways is invaluable for a leader and becomes more important the higher you go in your leadership career.

Having mentors is another way of getting the advice you need. Mentors aren't your parents, friends, or business colleagues. The "been-there-done-that" wisdom that mentors provide is an indispensable asset to improve your ability to lead, to advance in your career, and to provide leadership advice to others.

DEEPER INSIGHT

Your trusted advisers are your "personal board of directors." At best, they will backstop you when it comes to accountability. They will also furnish the perspective and knowledge you need to succeed and, not inconsequentially, to avoid unnecessary pain. Trusted advisers focus on the actual issues you face in the conduct of your duties.

Selecting a trusted adviser should be done carefully to ensure that you receive the specific expertise and support you need. The person you choose should have a deep understanding of his area of expertise, backed up by relevant credentials and demonstrated performance. He should understand your industry, your organization, and the challenges you face. He must be able to communicate his knowledge to you clearly and directly and challenge your assumptions without forcing his opinions on you. He should be a source of options, input, ideas, solutions, and rationale. Most important, your trusted adviser should be committed to the outcomes you seek and act in your best interest.

A mentor is someone, usually older, who has long experience in leadership in your industry. Mentoring is a developmental partnership in which the mentor shares knowledge, skills, information, and perspective in order to foster the personal and professional growth of a junior colleague. Mentoring relationships also provide a highly confidential way to share and explore problems, difficulties, and strategies for dealing with the challenges of leadership.

As you seek a mentor, look for someone you respect and whose career you would like to emulate. Make sure that person is willing to be a mentor, is willing to share her knowledge in an open way, and wants to support you in your career. It's also important that you trust your prospective mentor since you'll be sharing sensitive information about your organization, the people you work with, and yourself. Finally, pick a mentor you like, with whom you'll enjoy spending time.

Take the time up front to establish the basis for your relationship. Will it be formal or informal, scheduled or on an as-needed basis? How will you communicate—quick chats on the phone, e-mail, face to face, or all of the above?

★ ★ ★

Your trusted advisers and mentors will become your support team for leadership success. Choose them well!

RECAP

1. Trusted advisers and mentors are indispensable to your ongoing success as a leader.
2. Trusted advisers provide unfiltered feedback and input on the challenges you face so that you can make better decisions.
3. Mentors support you in your career development and are a sounding board for thoughts, ideas, and perspectives related to your particular leadership journey.
4. Choose your trusted advisers and mentors well. Carefully select them for their expertise, integrity, and compatibility.

SELF-COACHING QUESTIONS

1. Do I have trusted advisers and mentors?
2. If so, how well are those relationships working?
3. What are my criteria for selecting trusted advisers and mentors?
4. How can I improve my trusted adviser and mentor relationships?

INSIGHT #23

Losing a Battle but Not the War
Learning from Failure

"Failure is, in a sense, the highway to success, inasmuch as
every discovery of what is false leads us to seek earnestly after
what is true, and every fresh experience points out some form of
error which we shall afterwards carefully avoid."
—*Attributed to John Keats*

AFTER THE VIETNAM WAR, the US armed forces engaged in a
period of intense soul-searching as to what had gone wrong. The
conclusions drawn varied from "too much political interference"
to mismatched strategy to underestimating a resilient adversary.

In the ensuing years, a radical overhaul in organization, doctrine,
training, and equipping occurred in order to make sure that nothing
like Vietnam would ever happen again. The result of that transfor-
mation was seen in the destruction wreaked on Saddam Hussein's
forces during Operation Desert Storm.

Just as the United States did in Vietnam, during the course
of your leadership career, you will experience failure. What is

absolutely paramount is how you deal with failure. In fact, your future development and success hinge on the way you deal with it.

DEEPER INSIGHT

If you are in any way a perfectionist, a narcissist, ego-driven, hooked on personal glory, image conscious, or what in the Air Force is called a "fast-burner" (someone moving quickly up the ranks), you're going to have a hard time dealing with failure. In fact, you probably won't tolerate it well at all and, therefore, will miss the opportunity for personal growth and learning. For those who are willing to learn from failure, growth requires serious personal reflection and a willingness to understand what went wrong and why.

If you experience a failure for which you are responsible, the most important thing you can do is accept accountability. Don't run from it.

When I was in the Air Force, after an emergency response, an exercise, or a training event we used a series of tools to evaluate what went well and what went wrong. These tools, such as the after-action review, lessons-learned reports, and debriefings, were highly effective in mitigating or preventing failures when they were performed by capable leaders and received by open minds.

This doesn't mean that we were able to prevent all failures. What it does mean is that we took a deliberate approach to learning from our failures and putting processes, procedures, and training in place to avoid recurrences or, in the event of a repeat, to handle the situation better the next time.

Triage the failures. Don't just dismiss them out of hand. Try some fixes. See what you can salvage from them. In the process, you will learn more about what contributed to the failure and what it might take to generate success.

Another thing you can do is to create a knowledge-management system. Keep a collective memory of your failures alive so that you can draw on them in the future to inform your actions and decisions based on what you learned. Even more important, instill a culture in which people accept responsibility for failure and are willing to learn from it.

★ ★ ★

Dealing with the aftermath of failure is part of the process of achieving self-mastery—that deep awareness that comes from knowing who you are, what you stand for, and where your strengths and limitations lie. Learning and growing from failure will make you a more capable leader.

RECAP
1. Failure is part of leadership.
2. Learning from failure is essential to your growth and development as a leader.
3. Conduct after-action reviews following a failure.
4. Where practicable, triage your failures to see what else you might learn from them.
5. Create a culture of accountability for failure and a willingness to use it as a source of learning.

SELF-COACHING QUESTIONS
1. What have you learned from failure—your own or the failures of others?
2. How well do you tolerate failure in yourself and others?
3. How well does your organization or team tolerate failure?
4. Does the culture encourage you to share failures and what you have learned from them?
5. What, specifically, do you do to make sure you learn from failure?

INSIGHT #24

"Twelve O'Clock High"
Rebuilding Distressed Organizations

TWELVE O'CLOCK HIGH is a classic war movie that was shown for many years as part of Air Force Squadron Officer School (a school for younger officers) because of how well it teaches leadership lessons. In the movie, Gregory Peck plays Brigadier General Frank Savage, who is assigned to turn around the struggling 918th Bomb Group.

The 918th has gained a reputation as a hard-luck group after suffering severe losses during daylight precision bombing raids over Germany. Its previous commander, Colonel Frank Davenport, was relieved of command for poor performance and having become too close to his men.

With losses mounting and morale low, Savage takes on the job of turning the 918th into an elite unit, while simultaneously tasked with ongoing combat operations. Savage comes in like hell on wheels and deals with everyone, well, savagely.

In one of the classic scenes from the movie, Savage is riding in the front seat of his staff car as he arrives at the front gate of the base. He asks the driver to stop, gets out of the car, and paces nervously as he smokes a cigarette. Suddenly, he tosses the cigarette to the ground, gets in the back of the car, and tells the driver to pull up to the gate where the guard on duty nonchalantly waves him through. Savage then orders the driver to back up, chews out the guard for not following proper procedures, and demotes him on the spot.

Talk about making an entrance.

With the men on the verge of mutiny, Savage goes on to use a wide variety of tactics to coalesce the unit into a well-oiled fighting machine. Morale improves, as does combat performance. Savage succeeds under exceptionally trying conditions, but he does so at great personal cost to his health.

There may be times in your career when you find yourself leading an organization that is struggling. Like Savage, you'll need to find a way to turn things around, which may include severe, unpopular measures.

DEEPER INSIGHT

Rebuilding distressed organizations is perhaps the most difficult task a leader will ever undertake. Such organizations face unforgiving, volatile, and ambiguous environments. The pressure is enormous and the urgency of the task acute. To turn the organization around, you will need the utmost in professional acumen, communication and team-building skills, perseverance, and internal fortitude.

The harsh reality is that the organization won't change unless the leader has the skills, mindset, and resoluteness to make it happen.

Chief among your tasks will be to quickly diagnose what's going wrong and what's going right, and then to establish a clear vision of where the organization needs to go. This includes:

- Identifying the practices that are working and those that are not
- Establishing new values and practices
- Getting control of time, money, and resources to finance the rebuilding effort
- Making sure you have the right team in place
- Establishing a "triage plan" to keep the organization alive as you enact longer-range recovery actions
- Evaluating organizational structure, functions, and processes
- Assessing your people, including other leaders
- Keeping things as simple as possible to facilitate forward progress
- Keeping the promises you make

Also vital is your need to communicate the ongoing situation clearly, effectively, and appropriately to your organization. Leaders must craft and deliver hard-hitting, frank messages such as:

- How things used to be and why they are no longer that way
- What still works that you can built on
- The need for you to take responsibility for current issues, past and present mistakes, and future consequences
- The need for help from all members of the organization
- A compelling vision for the future
- How everyone can contribute to rebuilding the organization
- The urgency of the current situation

You must also communicate clear expectations to your leadership team regarding responsibilities, behavior, and performance toward the rebuilding effort. This relationship is particularly important to your overall success. The people in your organization must come to believe—or at least be willing to support—your vision and its implementation.

In order to drive and ensure implementation, you need a well-conceived, actionable, and measurable action plan.

The criteria for success are especially demanding. If you find yourself in a rebuilding situation, you are likely to feel harried and under pressure. Having the personal ability to deal with stress will help you preserve the cognitive, emotional, and physical resources you need to lead well.

★　★　★

Rebuilding a distressed organization requires a tremendous investment in time, energy, commitment, and engagement. In this turbulent environment, decisive decision making, close control and oversight, attention to detail, and stress resilience become the watchwords for success.

RECAP

1. Rebuilding distressed organizations is one of the hardest tasks a leader will face.

2. This challenge will require all of your talent, skill, and expertise.

3. Accomplishing a turnaround means that no stone can be left unturned, from finances to organizational structure to processes to human resources. Everything must be scrutinized for efficiency, effectiveness, and relevance.

4. The leader's communication with all members of the organization and external stakeholders throughout the rebuilding process is absolutely crucial to success.

5. It's important to manage your internal resources to cope with the stress inherent in any rebuilding effort.

SELF-COACHING QUESTIONS

1. In the case of a downturn, how well equipped are you in terms of your expertise, skills, and resilience?

2. What are the key signs of distress you should be aware of in your organization?

3. What contingency plans do you have in place in the event of organizational underperformance?

4. What lessons did you learn from being in other distressed organizations that you can apply to your current situation?

INSIGHT #25

Communicate Like Churchill
Inspire Through Authenticity

"We shall go on to the end. We shall fight in France, we shall fight
on the seas and oceans, we shall fight with growing confidence
and growing strength in the air, we shall defend our island,
whatever the cost may be. We shall fight on the beaches,
we shall fight on the landing grounds, we shall fight
in the fields and in the streets, we shall fight in the hills;
we shall never surrender."
—*Sir Winston Churchill, speech delivered to the House of
Commons of the Parliament of the United Kingdom, June 4, 1940*

IMMEDIATELY FOLLOWING THE SPEECH, the House of Commons erupted in a thunderous roar, and soon after the words were
pasted on the walls of offices and homes across the country.

With this single speech Churchill rallied a nation and an empire
in some of its darkest days—this just after its army had been
evacuated from the port at Dunkirk, narrowly avoiding destruction
by advancing German divisions.

DEEPER INSIGHT

While the oratory skills of Churchill are nearly impossible to attain, all leaders must be able to communicate effectively to all kinds of people and in all kinds of situations. Further, leadership studies have shown a direct correlation between a leader's success and his ability to communicate well.

As a leader, you are *always* communicating, whether or not you are speaking. Think of it as living in a glass fishbowl; be aware that everyone is watching you and evaluating you all the time. Much of your communication—80 percent, according to some research—is nonverbal. You convey volumes through your gestures, facial expressions, and posture.

In order to communicate with authenticity, you have to be perceived as genuine. This means you must be tuned in to the nature of the situation and what it demands of you. Are you coming across in a way that conveys your sincere thoughts and emotions? Or are you coming across as forced and "politically correct"?

Also, you must be aware of the verbal and nonverbal messages others are sending so that you can craft your message to their needs. In this way, you will connect with people more fully, since your words and your nonverbal cues will more closely correspond to what they are thinking and feeling.

Have you heard the expression, "He talks the talk but doesn't walk the walk."? When someone is described in this way, it means that his actions and words are incongruent. People instantly recognize a lack of authenticity.

When what you say and what you do are in sync, you are seen as authentic, genuine, and believable. To be seen as someone who "walks the walk," you must communicate a sense of trustworthiness and honesty. Of course, it helps immensely if you actually *are* trustworthy and honest. If not, your credibility and authority will be eroded, along with your ability to get things done. And getting things done is ultimately your primary function.

To communicate effectively, you need to listen without judgment, to really hear what is being said. Only if you pay close attention to the issues, concerns, and ideas that others bring up will you know how to respond appropriately. Listening is crucially important to building trust and enhancing credibility. The idea here is to strive at all times to be an "equal-opportunity listener" without letting your ego or your judgments get in the way.

Finally, when you actually do say something, make it count.

★ ★ ★

As Churchill did, prepare and practice your remarks before you deliver them. When you do, speak in language that those around you can perfectly understand. Know your audience, know what needs to be said, and then say it plainly in a way that resonates with your listeners.

RECAP

1. To be a great leader, you must be able to communicate well.
2. Realize that you are always communicating with your words, your body language, and your actions.
3. Be authentic when you communicate.
4. Really listen to your people.
5. Make your words count: know your audience, know what needs to be said, and speak in a way that will resonate with your listeners.

SELF-COACHING QUESTIONS

1. How do you rate your communication skills?
2. What are your communication strengths?
3. Where do you need to improve your communication skills?

4. How well do you listen?

5. How well are you able to communicate with different groups (e.g., front-line employees, peers, superiors, customers, the public)?

6. What can you do to improve your communication skills?

INSIGHT #26

"Under-the-Oak-Tree Counseling"
Build Trust with Your People

WHEN I WAS STATIONED in Korea as the commander of the communications squadron at Osan Air Base, the commanding general of US and UN forces on the peninsula was Army General Burwell B. Bell, known as "BB" Bell.

Every day when I got home and tuned in to Armed Forces TV, I was treated to General Bell talking about "under-the-oak-tree counseling"—his program to help reduce the risks and hazards associated with being in unfamiliar places. It was also a way to push leaders to get to know their soldiers and teach their subordinates how to conduct themselves when off-duty.

Bell insisted that leaders talk to their troops before "weekends, holidays, passes, leaves, and other identified periods of high risk." He directed that "first-line supervisors will meet with subordinates to discuss and set conditions for their off-duty plans."

Although the "under the oak tree" metaphor was a bit forced, the intent was pure: get to know your people through regular and sincere communication in order to build trust.

When trust does not exist between leaders and followers or within an organization, it's much more difficult to get even the smallest thing done. As Steven M. R. Covey (2006) wrote in *The Speed of Trust*, when trust goes up, speed goes up, and cost goes down. Trust has a practical impact on organizational performance as well.

There were times early in my career when I could have done a better job of building trust. Looking back, the main reasons I didn't were because I was too headstrong, didn't listen very well, and wasn't consistent in the way I made decisions. The result was that my people didn't know if they could put their trust in me.

Over the intervening years, I learned how to inspire trust and extend trust to others. I'm glad I did, because it made a positive difference not only in my job results but also in my personal job satisfaction.

DEEPER INSIGHT

Trust is "an individual's belief in and willingness to act on the basis of the words, actions, and decisions of another" (McAllister, 1995). There is a lot riding on a leader's ability to generate trust. Building trust enhances communication, improves cooperation, increases engagement, facilitates acceptance of goals and vision, and raises organizational and team performance.

Trust comprises two elements: calculus-based trust (CBT) and identification-based trust (IBT) (Lewicki, Wiethoff & Tomlinson, 2005). CBT is a pragmatic calculation that weighs the benefits of sustaining a relationship versus the cost of terminating it (Lewicki & Bunker, 1995).

IBT relates to your confidence that your interests will be protected and that the other person doesn't require much oversight (Lewicki & Bunker, 1996). Relationships based on IBT are characterized by a high degree of respect, loyalty, and obligation (Graen & Uhl-Bien, 1995).

Trust has several additional facets, including belief by followers that:

- The leader is willing to be vulnerable.
- The leader is reliable, honest, fair, benevolent, competent, and predictable.
- The leader's intentions are sincere.

In addition, these factors should be apparent:

- The leader is willing to risk that others may not fulfill expectations.
- There is a level of mutual and willing dependency between leader and followers to achieve successful outcomes.
- The leader demonstrates concern for the welfare of others.

Although most people are inclined to grant some level of "automatic" trust to others, the willingness to accept vulnerability evolves over the course of a relationship as ongoing, positive interactions deepen trust. In other words, it takes sustained effort to build and maintain trust.

Here are some things you can do to build trust, based on an excellent model of trust developed by a team of scholars led by Dr. Shawn Burke (2007):

- **Increase trust based on your ability.**
  - ▸ Set compelling direction that your people perceive as challenging, clear, and consequential.
  - ▸ Demonstrate the technical skill to deal effectively with your area of responsibility.
  - ▸ Build an organizational structure that establishes meaningful work, efficiently allocates resources, establishes standards of conduct, and creates effective teams.

▸ Understand what is going on around you.

▸ Maintain standards, and adhere to them yourself.

▸ Encourage adaptability, learning, and open communication.

- **Increase trust based on your compassion.**

  ▸ Show your people that you care.

  ▸ Learn how to coach your people.

  ▸ Demonstrate respect for your people by understanding and developing their strengths and helping them overcome their weaknesses.

  ▸ Create reward systems and opportunities for training and development.

  ▸ Ask your people what ought to be done, and include them in decision making.

  ▸ Be consistent in how you deal with people.

- **Increase trust based on your integrity.**

  ▸ Be accountable. Hold yourself and others accountable for their actions, both good and bad.

  ▸ Act according to your core values and the values of the organization.

  ▸ Be fair in the way you treat people and carry out your leadership responsibilities.

As you work to build and maintain trust, remember that people need to know it is safe to take appropriate risks and that you will have their backs if they happen to make a mistake. Keep in mind that the organizational climate influences trust—or the lack of it—particularly if policies are unfair or allow insufficient discretion for employee action.

★ ★ ★

Ultimately, when your people trust you, they will follow you. However, that trust is not automatically given. Whether it's through efforts like "under-the-oak-tree counseling" or by consistently demonstrating your leadership skill, compassion, and integrity, you have to earn it and keep earning it.

RECAP

1. The ability to build and maintain trust is a key leadership skill.

2. Trust is "an individual's belief in and willingness to act on the basis of the words, actions, and decisions of another."

3. Trust enhances individual performance, team performance, and organizational performance.

4. Two types of trust are based on transactional calculations of cost-benefit (calculus-based trust) and mutual respect, loyalty, and obligation (identification-based trust). Identification-based trust is the more powerful of the two.

5. You can build trust through your ability, your compassion, and your integrity.

SELF-COACHING QUESTIONS

1. How am I practicing behaviors that foster, encourage, and empower trust?

2. Where is trust lacking in my relationships, why is it lacking, and how can I instill it?

3. What are my strengths when it comes to building and maintaining trust?

4. How can I be more open with my people and consistently demonstrate my trustworthiness?

INSIGHT #27

"Dear Mrs. Ryan"
The Power of Empathetic Communication

IN THE MOVIE *Saving Private Ryan*, one of the closing scenes involves narration by General George Marshall reading the letter he wrote to Private Ryan's mother after Ryan survived the climactic battle at the end of the film. In his letter, Marshall included the following correspondence from President Abraham Lincoln to a mother who had lost five sons during the course of the Civil War:

Dear Madam,

I have been shown in the files of the War Department a statement of the Adjutant General of Massachusetts that you are the mother of five sons who have died gloriously on the field of battle. I feel how weak and fruitless must be any word of mine which should attempt to beguile you from the grief of a loss so overwhelming. But I cannot refrain from tendering you the consolation that may be found in the thanks of the Republic they died to save. I pray that our Heavenly Father may assuage the anguish of your bereavement, and leave you only the cherished memory of the loved and lost, and

135

the solemn pride that must be yours to have laid so costly a
sacrifice upon the altar of freedom.
Yours, very sincerely and respectfully,
A. Lincoln

The letter is widely regarded as one of Lincoln's greatest works, on a par with the Gettysburg Address and his second inaugural address. It is a sterling example of empathetic communication.

DEEPER INSIGHT

Empathetic communication both sympathizes with someone's situation and touches her heart in a sincere, genuine way. It conveys that you identify with her feelings and that you appreciate and understand what she is experiencing.

Communicating empathetically, whether by attentive listening, writing, or speaking, requires a degree of emotional intelligence on your part. The benefits are legion, including improved:

- Teamwork
- Trust
- Loyalty
- Openness
- Sharing of ideas and thoughts

Empathetic communication is the chief means by which you can cultivate authentic relationships and bring a human touch into the organization. This invigorates what otherwise might be an emotionless environment focused solely on performance-based efficiency.

Empathy comprises two elements:

- You understand and appreciate the other person's predicament or feelings.

- You communicate that understanding back to the person in a meaningful way.

Of course, your ability to communicate empathetically depends on the degree of empathy you possess. This characteristic demands a certain maturity, patience, presence, and attentiveness that are often at odds with the results-driven business world. Empathy requires you to not only listen carefully but also to observe. To be truly empathetic is to hear the words and sense the emotions behind those words.

We can borrow from the medical arena to provide a model of empathetic communication. Because doctors and nurses need to communicate with their patients in a way that is both sensitive and therapeutic, there's been a fair amount of attention given to these skills in the medical literature. The following five-step communication process draws from that research and serves as a guide:

- **Name the emotion or feeling.** "That must be frustrating to you."
- **Understand the emotion or feeling.** "Experiencing that kind of let down must be difficult."
- **Show respect and affirm.** "I'm impressed you've been able to keep up as well as you have despite the challenges you're facing."
- **Explore the emotion or feeling.** "Tell me more about your frustration."
- **Give support.** "How can I help you with these challenges?"

In order to employ empathetic communication, make sure you attend to what is unspoken as well as what is spoken. Give yourself time to think and set aside judgment. Avoid interpreting the person's situation, attempting to solve his problem, or simply repeating his words verbatim.

★ ★ ★

Communicating empathetically is ultimately a way of showing respect. It can play a vital part in establishing rapport with your people, supporting them, and showing your own humanity.

RECAP

1. Empathetic communication is a way of showing others that you understand their problems or feelings.

2. Empathetic communication is the chief means by which a leader cultivates authentic relationships.

3. Communicating empathetically improves teamwork, trust, loyalty, openness, and exchange of ideas.

4. You can learn to communicate empathetically by following a five-step process: (1) Name the feeling; (2) understand the feeling; (3) affirm the other person; (4) explore the feeling; and (5) support the other person.

5. Communicating empathetically is one way of demonstrating respect.

SELF-COACHING QUESTIONS

1. When one of your people has a problem or concern, can you truly empathize?

2. How do you rate your ability to communicate empathetically?

3. Where do you sense a weakness in your communication skills, and how can you overcome it?

INSIGHT #28

"Bad News Doesn't Get Better with Time"
Delivering Bad News

"BAD NEWS doesn't get better with time" was one of my key leadership tenets, especially when I was serving as a commander of a unit.

If bad news is not communicated in a timely and responsible fashion, the consequences can be dire. Withholding bad news can create a negative impact on production, safety, customer service, and the bottom line.

When I was commanding units in the Air Force, I had a policy of open communication of bad news. There were four reasons for this policy:

- First, it was a way of recognizing that things would not always go well, even though the intention was always to do our best.

- Second, when things did go wrong, I wanted to set up an environment in which people were not afraid to bring me bad news. I explained that by bringing it up, we would be able to put our collective minds together and deal with the situation, whatever it was.

- Third, I wanted to establish the expectation that telling the truth, along with accepting accountability for whatever had occurred, were always good courses of action. Stepping up and telling your boss that something went wrong is not an easy thing to do. It involves risk and apprehension. To mitigate these very natural feelings, I always promised not to shoot the messenger in the process. Most times I did pretty well with this promise.

- Fourth, I wanted to instill a climate of trust within the unit, the assurance that I had the backs of the airmen even if something didn't go quite right. With open communication that engendered a sense of trust, we'd be able to get through anything.

There were many times when I had to deliver bad news to bosses who were not as understanding. In fact, I could expect a pretty thorough ass-chewing right off the bat. Some were deserved, some not. Nonetheless, I always felt that delivering that news quickly and honestly was the right thing to do. After a few of these experiences, I developed some tactics that served me well on many occasions.

DEEPER INSIGHT

It's good to have a structured approach to help you prepare for delivering bad news. The structure will help you think through the situation, frame the problem, and analyze your audience. This will increase the chances of the recipient actually listening to what you have to say and taking appropriate action.

- The Direct Approach. The direct approach states the bad news up front. Use this method when the news is not particularly damaging or does not significantly affect the recipient, when the bad news may be ignored, when the culture endorses this style of communication, or when you must convey a sense of being in control of the situation.

- The Indirect Approach. With the direct approach, the bad news has more potential to upset the receiver or provoke a hostile reaction when it is unexpected, threatens a key relationship, or puts your boss at risk. With the indirect technique, the news will be more palatable if you first "prepare the battle space" and create a buffer that eases the impact of the news while still getting the message across.

- With either approach, it is important to understand your audience. What makes him tick? What's important to him? What language resonates (or not) with him?

- Construct your message with the following elements in mind:

  ▸ Start with the best news.

  ▸ If possible, work in some complimentary language about the recipient or audience.

  ▸ Establish a common frame of reference you can both agree on.

  ▸ The first three steps constitute the buffer.

  ▸ Only at this point do you present the facts of the situation.

  If warranted, follow this up with an apology if you are responsible for the situation that created the bad news and a proposal for how you plan to move forward and deal with the issue. In other words, don't hand off a problem without a solution.

  Whether you take the direct or indirect approach, the next steps are to plan your message; rehearse; and then select the time, place, and method of delivery.

  ★　★　★

  Invest time and effort in this structured approach, and you'll increase your chances of successfully delivering bad news.

RECAP

1. Bad news doesn't get better with time.

2. Don't delay the delivery of bad news.

3. Institute a policy of open communication that facilitates the prompt delivery of bad news by your team members.

4. Follow a structured approach to think through the situation, frame the problem, and analyze your audience in order to increase your chances of successfully conveying bad news.

SELF-COACHING QUESTIONS

1. What is my approach for delivering bad news?

2. When have I done this well? Not so well?

3. What went right or wrong with my approach?

4. How can I improve my ability to communicate bad news?

5. Do I encourage my subordinates to be honest and straightforward when they deliver bad news, or do I "shoot the messenger"?

INSIGHT #29

Commander's Intent
Empowering Your People to Adapt and Act

"No plan survives contact with the enemy."
—*Field Marshal Helmuth von Moltke*

DURING WORLD WAR II, the Allied invasion force meticulously rehearsed the D-Day landing and follow-on operations. Key to the effort was a precisely planned series of glider and parachute landings aimed at securing crucial inland points so that ground forces could advance rapidly.

However, the way the operation actually unfolded was not at all like the original plan. Paratroopers dropped into unmarked landing zones or nowhere near their planned targets, and gliders landed in the wrong areas. In army parlance, it was a nutroll, a chocolate mess, and FUBAR (f****d up beyond all recognition) all at once.

It appeared that a military disaster had occurred. Yet only hours later, the original military objectives were being accomplished by ad hoc units that were taking the fight to a highly organized and fierce German resistance.

How did this happen?

Certainly, the spirit, initiative, and purpose for which the Allied soldiers were fighting had something to do with it. From another perspective, the commander's intent for the operation had been communicated continuously throughout those long months of training. This allowed the landing force to regroup on the fly and proceed to achieve their designated objective.

DEEPER INSIGHT

According to US military doctrine, *commander's intent* is "a clear and concise expression of the purpose of the operation and the desired military end state that supports mission command, provides focus to the staff, and helps subordinate and supporting commanders act to achieve the commander's desired result without further order, even when the operation does not unfold as planned" (US Department of Defense, 2011).

More broadly, commander's intent is a way of crystallizing the essence of a plan in a way that everyone can easily understand. However, this statement is more than just public relations or corporate communications. It distills and synthesizes the leader's strategy, goal, or objective with a clear message that those responsible can understand and act on without much further guidance. Said another way, commander's intent describes the desired end state of organized action and focuses your people on what must be done to achieve success, even when the plan goes south.

Implicit in commander's intent is the trust the leader has in those who will do the work to achieve the strategy, goal, or objective. That trust allows people the freedom of action to make decisions "on the ground" and adapt to changing circumstances while still moving the plan forward.

Using the D-Day example, Allied leaders encapsulated the "why" and the "what" of the invasion in a concise statement that was verbally repeated to the soldiers of the invasion force in order to secure the success of the invasion in terms of specific military objectives. When the original plan disintegrated after the landing in France, soldiers on the ground adapted to the chaos, self-organized, and achieved the required objectives in line with the commander's intent.

As a leader, you write the commander's intent, which captures your understanding of the situation, what must be done and why, and the outcome you envision. It consists of the following elements:

- **The desired end state** – what you want the situation to be after the plan has been completed

- **The purpose of the plan** – the compelling reason why the work must be done

- **Assessment of the competitive situation** – a statement of the particular challenges facing the organization in the execution of the plan

- **A broad sketch of how the organization is to achieve the desired end state** – the overall strategy and activities involved, so that those executing the plan can see themselves in it

- **A statement of the risks** – the significant risk inherent in the strategy and where/when the leader is prepared to accept or not accept risk

Commander's intent is an exercise in focus and synthesis that distills what is most important about the challenge you face. To help you develop your intent, keep in mind the following two statements:

- If we do nothing else, we must_____.
- The single most important thing we must do is_____.

By way of example, here is the commander's intent written by General Norman Schwarzkopf before the start of Operation Desert Storm in 1990:

"We will offset the imbalance of ground combat power by using our strengths against his weakness. Initially execute deception operations to focus his attention on defense and cause incorrect organization of forces. We will initially attack into Iraq homeland using air power to decapitate his leadership, command and control, and eliminate his ability to reinforce Iraqi forces in Kuwait and Southern Iraq. We will then gain undisputed air superiority over Kuwait so that we can subsequently and selectively attack Iraqi ground forces with air power in order to reduce his combat power and destroy reinforcing units. Finally, we will fix Iraqi forces in place by feints and limited objectives attacks followed by armored penetration and exploitation to seize key lines of communications nodes, which will put us in a position to interdict resupply and remaining reinforcements from Iraq and eliminate forces in Kuwait." (US Department of Defense, 1992)

★ ★ ★

Writing your commander's intent helps you think through the content of the plan, create alignment with organizational goals, and then deliver that message powerfully. Once the intent is heard and understood, give your people the necessary freedom of action to make it happen.

RECAP
1. "No plan survives contact with the enemy."
2. Commander's intent is a way to prevent uncertainty and chaos by distilling the essence of your strategy, communicating it, and empowering your people to execute it.

3. The commander's intent statement consists of your desired end state, purpose, assessment of the competitive situation, a synopsis of the concept, and a statement of risks.

4. As a leader, the commander's intent is yours. Therefore, you write it.

SELF-COACHING QUESTIONS

1. How can I use commander's intent in my organization?

2. Can I convey my intent in a clear, concise manner that those responsible for implementation will understand and own?

INSIGHT #30

"Everything in War Is Simple, but the Simplest Thing Is Difficult"
No-Hassle Time Management

THIS CLASSIC QUOTE from Prussian General Karl von Clausewitz reflects his experience in warfare—where the confusion and friction that emerge from the chaos and destruction can turn the smallest task into an arduous, drawn-out trial.

Leadership of most organizations is certainly not warfare in the real sense. But the friction inherent in the job results from the meetings, problems, decisions, interruptions, crises, plans, and results that leaders regularly face.

The work never stops, and the fire hose is never turned off. Twenty-four hours in a day are inadequate to complete all that must be done. The leader nonetheless must lead and get the job done.

Time management, therefore, is an indispensable leadership skill. How you manage your time has ripple effects throughout the rest of your organization, as subordinates follow your lead.

DEEPER INSIGHT

A mountain of books has been written on the subject of time management, and it would be advisable for you to read one or two of them to help you put together a reliable system. Another alternative is to take a course in time management.

However, in lieu of self-study or a course, a few straightforward ideas can move you well along to gaining or improving this critical skill.

The first step to effective time management is that you must know your own tendencies. Are you organized or scattered? Do you prefer to plan out your to-dos or let the day flow? Do you naturally focus on the big picture or on details? Since the answers to these questions will affect how well you manage your time, be sure to explore these tendencies as part of your leadership sight picture.

Next, for a period of two workweeks, meticulously document what you do every fifteen minutes from the time you get up in the morning until you arrive home from work in the evening. Be detailed and thorough. The data you collect will provide the basis for a realistic analysis of how you use your time.

After you complete your log, ask yourself the following questions to determine how you might use your time more effectively:

- What strategic value did the action have in terms of a letter grade? (A, B, C, D, F)
- Did it have to be done, or could the task have been eliminated?
- Did it have to be done at that moment, or could it have waited?
- Who else could have done it? (Delegation is an excellent time saver and a way to involve the rest of your team.)
- Did it have to be done so well? Sometimes, perfect is the enemy of good enough. If all you're looking for is a rough idea, or it's the first draft of a report or presentation, an 80 percent or even 60 percent solution might be good enough. And it will save time.

Develop a list of ideas to save time, including the following:

- Reprioritize the task in terms of strategic value; then, do what's most important.
- Delegate the task to someone who should be doing it or has the expertise.
- Eliminate the task if it adds no value or is redundant.
- Do the task more efficiency, become more skilled at the process, or streamline the steps you take to complete it.
- Complete the task adequately, as opposed to perfectly. Ask yourself if perfection is necessary or if something less will suffice.

★ ★ ★

The goal of time management is to use your time as wisely as possible in the service of the strategy, goals, and tasks for which you are responsible. To do this, you must establish priorities and use the available time to maintain focus and achieve results.

RECAP

1. As a leader, time is your most precious commodity. Use it wisely.

2. Using your time well sets a tone for your organization; it conveys the message that time is important.

3. Read books or take a course on time management to help you develop this indispensable leadership skill.

4. In order to learn time management, you need to (1) know your own tendencies, (2) analyze your habits, (3) follow a time-management process, and (4) continuously seek to improve your efficiency.

SELF-COACHING QUESTIONS

1. How well do I manage my time now?

2. What are my time-management tendencies?

3. What do I do well, and what do I do poorly when it comes to managing my time?

4. What are the consequences of my poor time management or the positive outcomes of my mastery of this skill?

5. How are my time-management skills (or my lack of them) affecting my team?

6. What are some things I can do to improve the way I manage time?

7. What kind of example am I setting for others?

INSIGHT #31

The Stand-Up
How to Run Great Meetings

I ENCOUNTERED MY FIRST stand-up meeting as a young lieutenant assigned to a communications group in Germany. Every morning, all the officers and key enlisted members were required to attend this highly structured, stand-and-deliver meeting with the very crusty—and very smart—colonel who ran the group. I learned quickly that it paid to be prepared because the colonel would bear down on you if you didn't have your stuff together, and sometimes even if you did.

I had a hate-love relationship with these meetings. I hated that knot of fear that formed in my stomach in anticipation of getting my rear-end handed to me; but I loved that the meetings were incredibly effective at eliciting the information the leadership team needed to deal with problems and make decisions very quickly and efficiently.

These stand-ups didn't waste anyone's time—especially the colonel's! There was no idle chitchat; everyone was on point and engaged. As a result, when the meeting ended, we walked out with a clear idea of the day's objectives with a minimum investment of time.

Later in my career, I remembered those stand-ups and vowed never to waste my folks' time with unnecessary meetings—and when I did have meetings, to make them count. I made it a point to keep my meetings focused, structured, and outcome-oriented, even if the meeting involved a discussion or coordination that would not lead to a decision. I found this method to be particularly successful when I worked at the Pentagon, which housed a formidable bureaucracy.

The process I used at the Pentagon tapped into a need for military and civilian "action officers" to actually take some action and do their jobs. These professionals always knew they would be doing something substantial when they participated in my meetings. *Meeting* and *efficiency* were two words that weren't spoken together at the Pentagon. So people appreciated that I respected their time.

The impact that my approach had on my ability to get things done was amazing.

DEEPER INSIGHT

Running a great meeting requires deliberate intent and focus. Some things to keep in mind include:

- Make a list of the required and optional participants.
- Construct and distribute a logical, time-driven schedule of events so everyone knows how to prepare.
- Make a list of deliverables and products required before the meeting, and set a deadline and format for their delivery.
- Reserve a room that is conducive to what you intend to accomplish.

- If time allows, send out multiple announcements to the participants, and secure their RSVPs. Follow up with phone calls if necessary.
- Introduce the meeting's host at the start of the meeting.
- State your purpose, objective, or desired outcome at the beginning of the meeting.
- Appoint your note taker.
- Keep the meeting flowing and on schedule. If a discussion can't be concluded, table it for a future meeting or an off-line discussion.
- Keep a tight handle on irrelevant topics and rabbit holes.
- Before concluding the meeting, sum up the tasks, agreements, outcomes, deliverables, responsible parties, and due dates. This is extremely critical so that everyone is clear as to what transpired and who will do certain tasks.
- Agree on a time, date, and location for the next meeting.
- No later than twenty-four hours after the meeting, send out meeting notes to all participants.

★ ★ ★

This may seem like a lot to go through, and it is when you first begin this process. However, I can assure you that it is a very effective approach to running both formal and informal meetings at any level of the organization. And as a side benefit, people will appreciate you for your outcome-oriented focus and your respect for their time.

RECAP

1. Run poorly, meetings can be huge time-wasters for you and your organization.

2. Conducting crisp and on-point meetings goes a long way toward keeping people engaged and achieving results.

3. Follow a proven process to prepare for, run, and follow up to your meetings.

4. Running tight, focused meetings demonstrates respect for your people and their time.

SELF-COACHING QUESTIONS

1. How do I rate my ability to run meetings?

2. How much preparation do I put into running good meetings?

3. What is my process for preparing for and running meetings?

4. What can I do to improve the efficiency, flow, and results of meetings?

5. Do I solicit feedback from meeting attendees? If I receive feedback, do I act on it?

INSIGHT #32

"Adapt, Improvise, Overcome"
Coaching Your Team

CLINT EASTWOOD'S PORTRAYAL of Master Gunnery Sergeant Tom Highway in the movie *Heartbreak Ridge* depicted him as a battle-hardened, old marine at odds with his chain of command. Charged with whipping a platoon of marine misfits into shape, Gunny Highway establishes basic discipline, teaches combat skills, and instills pride and morale through hard-nosed but time-tested military training methods.

In one of the iconic scenes in the movie, Gunny Highway is striding through the barracks before the crack of dawn while "motivating" his marines with colorful barbs interspersed with lines about what it means to be a marine and how to survive in combat.

One piece of wisdom instructed the marines to "adapt, improvise, and overcome" when faced with challenging circumstances in combat. Later in the movie, that is exactly what Gunny Highway's marines had to do, and that is what they did.

I don't recommend Gunny Highway's methods as part of your leadership style. But I do admire how, in his own particular way, he coached his men on how to be successful as a team in their environment, which happened to be combat.

For my part, I discovered coaching late in my Air Force career. As I pursued training as a coach, I was increasingly able to apply my new coaching skills to real situations of the airmen who reported to me. The results were nothing short of amazing. Performance improved as did my airmen's learning, development, professional growth, and self-confidence. This was very gratifying, to say the least. My only regret was that I had not learned how to coach much earlier in my career.

DEEPER INSIGHT

Fundamentally, coaching is the process of guiding and encouraging team members to achieve superior performance results. Coaching does not involve outright control or giving direction as most leaders are wont to do. Rather, a coach facilitates and supports the team as its members *discover for themselves* how to solve problems, grow, and develop.

In order to do this, as a coach, you must work with the team as a whole and with each individual team member to set up opportunities for learning and development. The heart of coaching is using powerful questions to trigger insight, growth, and success.

Here is a set of solution-focused questions you can use to help a team member who is trying to solve a problem:

- Coach employee to identify a solution.
  - ▸ What would you like to see happen?
  - ▸ What do you believe is the solution?
  - ▸ What is the ideal situation?

- Coach employee to identify a current and a future state.
  - ▸ In terms of the ideal situation, where are you now?

- ▸ On a scale of one to ten (with ten indicating best), where are you now?
- ▸ On that scale, where would you like to be?
- ▸ Is that a realistic goal?
- ▸ What strengths did you draw on to get this far?
- ▸ What is in place that is already working toward the ideal?
- Coach employee to identify the actions she needs to take.
  - ▸ What are the actions you can take right away? Tomorrow?
  - ▸ Who should be involved?
  - ▸ How will you coach and develop your people to engage them in this solution?

Such a solutions-focused coaching approach—when conducted with empathy, support, and patience—is extremely effective in helping people find their own solutions as they learn along the way.

For most leaders, the coaching approach will have to be learned and developed, since it so radically different from the way leaders are taught to lead. Going from controlling, driving, and directing to facilitating, encouraging, and partnering is not natural behavior for most leaders.

However, the benefits to the organization can be substantial, including:

- More effective teams
- Higher morale
- Better results
- Increased retention
- Improved customer service
- Higher productivity
- Greater adaptability

Your organization will derive the greatest benefit from coaching if this approach becomes a part of the culture.

A coaching culture has the following characteristics:

- Coaching is practiced by all organizational members, including leaders and teams.
- Coaching is the default method of supporting others and solving problems.
- The results of coaching help to increase the organization's revenues.

If you choose to build a coaching culture, realize that it will take time and a step-by-step process of implementation.

- Bring in a team of external coaches.
- Develop an organizational coaching strategy that links to your business strategy.
- Build internal coaching capacity.
- Cultivate, support, and encourage coaching at all levels of the organization.
- Embed coaching in your performance-management processes.
- Make coaching the predominant leadership style.
- Use coaching to interact and do business with all stakeholders.

★ ★ ★

Coaching generates supportive, solutions-focused conversations that stimulate thinking and reveal previously elusive options. Ultimately, coaching helps the organization and its people to be successful. As Bob Nadelli, former CEO of Home Depot, said, "I absolutely believe that people, unless coached, never reach their maximum capabilities."

Like Gunny Highway, do your part to help your people reach their potential, and do it by being a great coach.

RECAP

1. Coaching is a proven way to help your people solve problems, create results, and grow.
2. Coaching is a skill that must be learned and honed over time.
3. Powerful questions, empathy, active listening, and support are essential components of successful coaching.
4. Coaching can be extremely beneficial to the organization by helping to increase organizational communication, efficiency, and effectiveness.
5. A coaching culture helps people reach their potential.

SELF-COACHING QUESTIONS

1. How well am I able to coach one of my team?
2. What are my strengths and weaknesses as a coach?
3. Would I be willing to undergo training to improve my coaching skills?
4. How open am I to being coached?
5. How willing am I to introduce coaching in my organization? If I am not willing, why not?

INSIGHT #33

"The Snowstorm Has Stopped"
Ask Powerful Questions

"Judge a man by his questions rather than his answers."
—*Voltaire*

WHEN I WAS stationed at the Pentagon, I worked on the Joint Staff in support of then chairman, General Peter Pace. The secretary of defense at the time was Donald Rumsfeld, who had a well-deserved reputation for being tough and extremely demanding.

Secretary Rumsfeld's legendary management style involved what were known as "snowflakes"—hand-written or dictated memos. They could be short or lengthy; their tone could be complimentary or hectoring; and the topics could range from the insignificant to the truly momentous.

Rumsfeld observed: "Snowflakes quickly became a system of communication with the many employees of DoD [the Department of Defense], as I would initiate a topic with a short memo to the relevant person, who would in turn provide research, background, or a course of action as necessary."

Here's a snowflake that refers to the procurement of armored personnel carriers for Iraq and Afghanistan security forces:

"February 28, 2005
TO: Paul Wolfowitz
FROM: Donald Rumsfeld
SUBJECT: Armored Personnel Carriers
   Attached is a paper on a Slovenian armored personnel carrier. There are a variety of these floating around the world.
   My question is this: If we need more armored vehicles, why don't we buy them instead of trying to make them faster than people apparently can make them? If other people need them, and are going to need them, like the Iraqi Security Forces or the Afghan Security Forces, shouldn't they have that in their budgets? Please focus in on this, and get back to me with a report as to what you recommend, if anything.
   Thanks."

From a leadership standpoint, the snowflakes were emblematic of an experienced executive who knew how to ask powerful questions in a bureaucracy skilled at avoiding answering them.

DEEPER INSIGHT

Being able to ask powerful questions is a true hallmark of a mature leader. Not only does it take breadth and depth of experience and a comprehensive understanding of the organization, it also requires that the leader excel at unpacking the complexity of thorny problems and penetrating to their essence. It means asking questions that provoke new—even surprising—ways of thinking and reframing standard problems in ways that provide increased understanding of different perspectives.

Asking powerful questions:

- Inspires the respect and trust of subordinates
- Teaches subordinates to solve tough problems for themselves
- Requires patience because sometimes you ask questions to which you already know the answer, or you receive answers that don't quite hit the mark
- Calls for a shift in thinking of the leader as the "smartest one in the room" to viewing the leader as a coach or teacher—not an easy change for those who are used to calling the shots

A powerful question is one that:

- Stimulates reflective thinking
- Challenges assumptions
- Provokes thought
- Generates insight
- Opens avenues for inquiry
- Probes for deeper meaning
- Evokes more questions
- Is open-ended rather than closed-ended (*What do you plan to do about your professional development?* as opposed to *Are you going to do something about your professional development?*)
- Begins with interrogative words, such as how, what, when, where, why, and which
- Uses the conditional tense rather than the definitive tense (*What could we do?* instead of *What can we do?*)
- Is broad in scope and content (*How should we manage the company?* is more powerful than *How should we manage our sales force?*)

- Helps reframe the way the problem is viewed and shifts the context (*How can we collaborate with the industry leaders?* rather than *How can we compete with industry leaders?*)

★ ★ ★

Asking powerful questions is a learned skill, and like other skills, it takes practice. The payoff is worth the effort. By doing so, you increase the quality of communication between you and your people, generate more effective courses of action, and teach the skill to others by modeling it.

RECAP

1. Asking powerful questions is the hallmark of a mature, confident leader.

2. Powerful questions can help leaders unpack complex problems and open new avenues of understanding.

3. Powerful questioning also inspires respect and trust from subordinates and teaches them to be critical thinkers.

4. Like any other skill, being able to ask powerful questions takes practice, but the payoff is worth it in terms of the benefit to your organization and your people.

SELF-COACHING QUESTIONS

1. What are the benefits of powerful questioning for me and my people?

2. How can I incorporate powerful questions into my day-to-day leadership practices?

3. What are some ways I can improve my ability to ask powerful questions?

INSIGHT #34

Spartans at Thermopylae
Inculcating Esprit de Corps

THE STORY OF THE SPARTANS turning back the great Persian army at Thermopylae, the "Hot Gates," was immortalized by the Greek historian Herodotus and more recently the subject of the movie *300*. The bravery of the Spartans and their allies is truly the stuff of legend.

Although the Greeks lost the battle at Thermopylae, the way they embraced their duty captures the concept of esprit de corps: a sense of commitment and zeal that binds you to your teammates and cements your commitment to the organization's mission.

DEEPER INSIGHT

A sense of organizational spirit arises from the transcendent "why" of your work and reinforces the purpose of the organization. It gives members a sense of healthy pride in their contribution, no matter how large or small or what their level or role in the organization.

This ethos of engagement is fundamental to successful organizations. An engaged employee is fully involved in his work, thus furthering the organization's mission. In contrast, a disengaged employee lowers morale and costs the company market share and money.

Research has also shown that an engaged workforce leads to retention of talent, better customer service, stronger individual performance, increased team performance, higher business-unit productivity, and greater financial results.

Some of the drivers of engagement include:

- Involvement in decision making
- Extent to which employees feel able to voice their ideas and the manager's willingness to listen to and value these ideas
- Opportunities for employees to develop in their jobs
- Organizational concern for employees' health and well-being
- Employee perceptions of job's importance
- Employee clarity on job expectations
- Career advancement and improvement opportunities
- Regular feedback and dialogue with boss
- Quality working relationships between peers, superiors, and subordinates
- Effective communication
- Well-calibrated reward systems

From my experience in the military service, the organizations with the highest esprit de corps were the ones in which:

- The purpose of the organization was clear.
- The mission was both compelling and fulfilling.
- All airmen could find their places in the mission.

- All airmen felt valued and appreciated for what they did by their chain of command as well as their peers.

- Overcoming shared struggle gave rise to strong relationships and bonds of trust and friendship, as well as true pride in service.

- Where history and tradition, particularly of the organization's past successes and contributors, were remembered.

Esprit de corps inspires pride, belonging, purpose, and trust. It assures people that they matter and what they do for the organization matters. It provides the internal psychic energy for people to internalize the mission of the organization, align with the culture and strategy, and commit to success. In an organization with esprit de corps, people enjoy their work; they readily do more than asked; and they become proactive, persistent, and adaptable. An organization with esprit de corps cracks with urgency, focus, intensity, and enthusiasm.

I was fortunate to have served in several of these organizations in which the sense of trust, fulfillment, loyalty, friendship, and pride we all felt was second to none. We worked hard, enjoyed each other's company, supported each other, and flat worked our tails off to be successful. That feeling was something I never wanted to lose, but once it was gone, I found myself looking for a way back into a unit that had it or would work to create it.

★ ★ ★

Inculcating organizational spirit is something that a leader can and should strive to do. Although leadership is indispensable and in many cases decisive in creating organizational spirit, this endeavor is ultimately a team sport. The whole organization must be committed in order to fully achieve and sustain esprit de corps.

Worth aspiring to? In my opinion, absolutely!

RECAP

1. Esprit de corps is a hallmark of elite organizations.

2. When organizational spirit is high, it gives rise to a sense of commitment and zeal that binds you to your teammates and makes your service to a mission worthwhile.

3. Esprit de corps inspires people to do more than asked; commit to the organization's success; and be proactive, persistent, and adaptable.

4. Creating organizational spirit is a team sport; everyone contributes to making the organization elite.

SELF-COACHING QUESTIONS

1. When have I experienced high esprit de corps in my career?

2. What was it about that organization that caused me to commit to it?

3. Does my current organization exhibit high esprit de corps? Why or why not?

4. What opportunities are there for improvement?

5. What are some ways I can increase the esprit de corps in my team and in my organization?

INSIGHT #35

Giving Your Best Military Advice
Managing Your Boss

AS A RESULT of the Goldwater-Nichols Act of 1986, the chairman of the Joint Chiefs of Staff became the senior uniformed military officer of the US armed forces. In this role, the chairman is the principal military adviser to the president, the National Security Council, and the secretary of defense.

Although the chairman has no direct operational control of forces in the field or the military services, by virtue of his legal authority and direct connection to the president, he exercises tremendous influence in matters of military strategy and resource allocation.

To utilize, retain, and even grow this influence, the chairman must establish credibility not only with the president but also with the senior civilians of the Department of Defense, ranking military officers, members of Congress, and leaders of other government departments. To be sure, being effective in this job is a constant balancing act that requires an exceptionally well-developed political sense.

However, the chairman's primary relationship is with the president; this is where the rubber meets the road in terms of influence. Every interaction must be purposeful, with an appropriate mix of forthrightness, nuance, and context.

Certainly, the chairman does not seek to control or "manage" the president; nonetheless, it is critical that he understand the president in terms of personality, thinking, and decision-making style; preferences for taking in information; hot buttons; and agenda.

As my military career progressed, I realized how important it was for me to (1) establish credibility with my bosses, (2) keep my bosses appropriately informed, (3) help them make the best decisions possible, and (4) become indispensable to my bosses. Sometimes, this was easy and straightforward; other times, it was difficult and painful. But either way, I had a responsibility to provide my best advice.

DEEPER INSIGHT

Like the chairman of the Joint Chiefs of Staff, you have a boss. Even if you're a CEO, you have the board of directors as your boss.

As much control as you might have, that control is always dependent in some way on your boss. In order to offer "your best military advice," it's important to understand what makes your boss tick—to seek to understand her at a deeper level. Some questions to consider along these lines are:

- How does your boss define success in her professional career?
- How does she define success in her role?
- What are her specific career goals and aspirations?
- What are her most important performance goals and initiatives?
- How does she define personal success?
- What are her specific personal goals and aspirations?

- What is her communication style?
- What is her tolerance for risk and change?
- How does she make decisions (e.g., from a financial, technical, political, aesthetic, or other perspective)?
- What drives and motivates her to succeed?
- What behaviors on the part of employees and colleagues are sure to upset her?
- How does she prefer to take in information?
- How would you characterize her boss's personality?

It's also necessary to be on point when you interact with your boss. Treat conversations, briefings, and encounters with the professionalism they deserve. Always be prepared and try to understand the context of the situation at the moment. If the interaction is particularly important, take the time to structure and rehearse your approach to achieve maximum effect. Consider the following questions before the meeting:

- What is your objective or desired outcome?
- What do you want him to do, think, or feel?
- How will you open the conversation?
- How do you think he will respond?
- What objections and concerns might he raise?
- What will you say to show that you have heard and acknowledge his issues?
- What questions can you ask to more fully understand his position and interests?
- What other approach can you make in case your first strategy fails to work or new information emerges that you hadn't considered?
- What can you do during the meeting to be sure that the place, time, and other factors make him feel comfortable?

- What could go wrong in this meeting (e.g., emotions, new facts coming to light)?
- What will you do if things go from bad to worse?
- How will you excuse yourself and reschedule for another time?

Another valuable strategy is to have an impact on others who have influence with your boss. You can use the same questions as above to help with that, but be sure to ask the following questions as well to assess the efficacy of such an approach:

- To what degree does the potential influencer have leverage on the issue at hand?
- What is the influencer's position on the issue?

Your influence, in large part, depends on the strength of your relationship with your boss. This doesn't mean you have to be drinking buddies, but it does mean that you must have a healthy professional relationship based on mutual respect and that you can openly share thoughts, ideas, and opinions. No other relationship is as important, and the best way to assess this is to ask yourself some soul-searching questions. The following questions will help you with that assessment and, in fact, might make you very uncomfortable. Your answers might also surprise you.

- What does your boss expect you to achieve?
- What must you do well to meet her expectations?
- How would she say you are performing?
- How does she expect you to communicate progress, issues, and results?
- How well would she say you communicate with her?
- How much trust and confidence would you say she has in you? How do you know?
- How well would she say that you adapt to her style of communicating, working, and making decisions? Why does she think that?

- How committed are you to helping her succeed on both professional and personal levels? Would she agree?
- What, if any, past issues remain unresolved between the two of you?
- How can you resolve those issues or make amends?
- Would you rate her as a mentor: supportive, neutral, negative, or strongly negative toward you?
- Overall, how would you rate your professional relationship with her?
- How would you rate your personal relationship with her?

Once you've completed your assessment of your relationship, it's time to develop a plan to strengthen it or, if it's good, to maintain it. The following questions are designed to help you do either one:

- How willing are you to strengthen the relationship and make it work even better?
- What do you need to ask him to find out more about how you are performing?
- What can you do to help him look better in the organization?
- What can you do to prevent him from looking bad in the organization?
- What can you do to help him have more time to pursue his primary professional and personal interests?
- What can you do to communicate more effectively with him?
- How can you better adapt your style to work more effectively with his style?
- How can you clear up any past issues or mistakes that have occurred between you and him?
- What judgments about him can you overcome to strengthen the relationship?

- What, if anything, can you do to increase the level of trust, respect, and confidence he has in you?
- How can you improve your personal relationship with him?
- What requests do you need to make of him to improve your performance—without making him seem or feel like he is in the wrong?
- How can you better communicate the value you bring to him and the organization without being impertinent?

★ ★ ★

This section has gone deep into the dynamics of the most important relationship you have as a leader. If you've answered the questions sincerely, no doubt you've realized that you must continually invest in this relationship to make it as mutually beneficial and productive as it can be, especially in terms of your ability to influence your boss.

RECAP

1. No matter what your leadership level, you're always going to have a boss.
2. It's vital to your success, your boss's success, and the success of the organization that you be able to manage up.
3. Seek to have a productive relationship with your boss. In order to do this, you need to understand her motivations, pressures, fears, and aspirations.
4. Always work to strengthen your relationship with your boss by figuring out ways to help her.

SELF-COACHING QUESTIONS

1. How would I characterize my relationships with my current and previous bosses?

2. What are the patterns of interaction in these relationships? Are they positive or negative patterns?

3. How well do I know my boss?

4. How strong is my relationship with my current boss?

5. What are some ways I can strengthen that relationship?

INSIGHT #36

The Incredible Initiative of Airman Lateer
Leading from Below

DURING MY LAST TOUR in the Air Force, I served as the commander of a communications unit whose mission was to deploy "anytime, anywhere" to set up voice and data networks in support of Air Force field operations. As a result of looming budget cuts and force reductions, we were putting a lot of emphasis on innovation and new ways of doing business. We also wanted to instill the drive to innovate all the way down to the newest airman in the unit and make it a part of our warrior ethos. Nowhere are innovation and the ability to adapt more important than in war.

We had one young airman named Lateer who had just returned from a deployment in Afghanistan. There, he had been placed in charge of setting up and running a communications network on an Afghani air force training base near the Iranian border in the western part of the country. To say the conditions there were primitive would be an understatement. To complicate matters, he and the rest of his team were coming under regular insurgent rocket attack—and they were the defense force.

Despite these challenges, Airman Lateer and the rest of the team built the communications network that supported the US Air Force, US Army, NATO, and Afghani forces on the base. However, Airman Lateer had found that a gap in his training made it more difficult for him to do his job. He wanted to do his best for the mission, so this bothered him greatly.

After his deployment ended, Airman Lateer resolved to fix this situation. He subsequently invested a great deal of time figuring out ways to deliver the training he and his fellow airmen needed to be successful in complex and dangerous expeditionary deployments.

Now, you have to understand the audacity of this undertaking. In the Air Force, young airmen are implementers of decisions. If they have ideas, they usually have to get approval from several layers of supervision before moving forward. The process is far more difficult than it needs to be. But Airman Lateer was undeterred. What started with an idea born of his experience turned into a revolutionary approach to training his fellow airmen that employed a virtual simulator for all of the tasks required to maintain and defend a deployed network.

The capability he created used existing resources and equipment for little or no cost. Not only that, he put together a show-and-tell briefing for his chain of command that ultimately resulted in my endorsement as well as that of the two-star commander in charge of the Air Force's cyber command.

Talk about leading from below!

DEEPER INSIGHT

Airman Lateer used several techniques to lead from below.

- **Establish credibility:** First and foremost, through his performance and attitude in the field, he had established a strong level of professional credibility. This gave him an authoritative platform far beyond his rank from which to move forward.

- **Solve an important problem:** He identified a significant problem that needed to be solved. Long-term sustainment of deployed communications networks was a stated issue that leadership wanted to address.

- **Understand your boss:** He understood his bosses, what they needed, and how to help them.

- **Communicate effectively:** He knew how to communicate with his bosses in a way that resonated with them and gained their support.

- **Follow through:** Ultimately, Airman Lateer was able to form a team of peers and experts to develop a capability that actually worked. He then put together a comprehensive training plan and won approval to distribute it throughout the combat communications community of nearly four thousand airmen across the world.

Leadership guru Marshall Goldsmith and his coauthors (2004) offer these guidelines for leading up.

- When presenting your ideas, realize that it is your responsibility to sell, not leadership's responsibility to buy.

- Focus on contributing to the larger good, not just achieving your objectives.

- Strive to win the big battles; don't waste your energy and psychological capital on trivial points.

- Present a realistic cost-benefit analysis of your ideas; don't just sell benefits. All organizations have limited resources. The acceptance of your idea may well mean the rejection of another idea that someone else believes is wonderful.

- Take the high road on issues involving ethics or integrity. Ethics violations can destroy even the most valuable companies.

- Realize that your upper managers are just as human as you are. It is realistic to expect upper managers to be competent; it is unrealistic to expect them to be better than normal human beings.

- Treat senior leaders with the same courtesy that you would treat partners or customers. Avoid kissing up, but also avoid being disrespectful.

- Support the final decision of the team. Assuming that the final decision of the team is not immoral, illegal, or unethical, go out and try to make it work.

- Make a positive difference; don't just try to win or be right.

- Focus on the future, and let go of the past.

★ ★ ★

You will always have a boss. The art of being able to lead from below is a necessary skill for gaining support and resources, getting things done, and achieving results.

Emulate Airman Lateer: establish credibility, understand your boss, communicate well, and follow through on what you say. In so doing, you may not win them all, but you will win your share.

RECAP

1. Leading from below is the ability to sell your ideas to your superiors and enlist them to help you get them implemented.

2. Leading from below is an important leadership skill and an art rather than a science.

3. It takes courage, commitment, and perseverance to lead from below.

4. To be successful at leading from below you must (1) be credible, (2) solve an important problem, (3) understand your boss, (4) communicate effectively, and (5) follow through.

SELF-COACHING QUESTIONS

1. What are some times when I have successfully led from below?

2. What made me successful?

3. How effective am I at leading from below in my current position?

4. How can I improve my ability to lead from below?

5. In what ways do I encourage my people to lead from below?

6. How do I support my people when they bring me their ideas?

INSIGHT #37

Building Future Leaders
Succession Planning

THE AIR FORCE and other military services invest a lot of time, effort, and money in developing leaders. The US armed forces operates using an all-volunteer, up-or-out model. This means that those who join want to serve, but not all who deserve to get promoted *are* promoted.

Given this structure and the needs of military service, career development teams are used throughout a member's career to build experience, increase knowledge, and strengthen leadership capability. This approach creates an internal reserve of leaders to step in if the ranks need to be increased. It also generates leaders to run the massive US military bureaucracy during peacetime and fight the nation's battles when called on during times of war.

The result is that when it comes time to have soldiers, sailors, airmen, and marines ready to move to the senior leadership ranks, the military services find themselves blessed by an embarrassment of riches.

As a product of the military system of succession planning, I benefited from structured career development and participated in it to make it work. From a professional standpoint, the variety of assignments, positions, schooling, and training I received was directly responsible for whatever leadership acumen I displayed over the years. And, as one who helped develop future leaders, I appreciated the investment of time, resources, and expertise available to me to give those up-and-coming service men and women what they needed to become successful leaders in their own right.

DEEPER INSIGHT

At its core, succession planning ensures the ongoing viability of an organization and the availability of a ready pool of leadership talent. It is a way of continually adapting to the changing organizational environment by assessing and deepening the "leadership bench." An organization with a strong succession planning process identifies high-potential leaders, and through a systematic series of assignments, projects, training, and education, prepares them for advancement up the ranks.

Succession planning starts with a strategic understanding of where the market and organization are heading and anticipating the future talent needed to fill critical leadership roles. Important questions for leaders to ask in this regard include:

• What strategic drivers are creating new needs for our organization?

• Which leadership roles will continue to be important? Which will not?

• What new talents, skills, and expertise will be critical as the organization adapts, evolves, and grows?

• What new leadership roles do we need to develop and fill?

- Who will be retiring or leaving in the near future?
- Who are our potential successors?
- What is our process and plan to make succession occur efficiently and effectively?

To engage in effective succession planning, it is vital for an organization to identify what roles are important and what is going on with the incumbents in those roles (moving up, looking to retire or leave, etc.). Then, each key role should be assessed in terms of responsibilities, authority, key talents and skills needed, and specific performance metrics required to do well in the role.

The next critical task in succession planning is to map out a career path so that senior leaders and those wishing to move up in the organization are clear about what is necessary.

The organization then must concretely involve its leaders for professional growth and development. Development plans are a typical way of doing this, but formal and informal mentorship and coaching are also very beneficial. Regular performance appraisals and reviews are indispensable in assessing how potential leaders are progressing.

If an organization brings leadership in from the outside, it must have a clear recruiting process and standards in order to hire the right talent, bring that person on board, and orient the newly hired leader as quickly and smoothly as possible.

Two often-overlooked aspects of succession planning are identifying "flight risks" and transferring knowledge from incumbents to successors.

Ideally, flight risks—people who are looking for opportunities outside the organization—should be identified as part of the development-and-performance-assessment process. A good succession-planning process will flag these people for additional engagement in order to formulate a plan to retain them.

Knowledge transfer can be a tricky thing to pull off, especially with incumbents who have been in a position for a while and may not be keen on passing essential elements of their knowledge. Key skills, informal knowledge of "how things get done around here," and networks of contacts are all important to consider when it comes to knowledge transfer.

★ ★ ★

Succession planning, when executed well, ensures that you have leaders with the necessary experience, skills, and knowledge to step up and fill leadership roles in the company when the time is right. You need only look at the US military to see this concept in practice. Like the military, be sure you have leaders waiting in the wings to run your organization.

RECAP

1. Succession planning helps ensure development of the leadership you need to run your organization and keep it viable for the long term.

2. A good succession-planning process starts with a survey of the strategic position of your organization and the kind of leadership it needs to achieve its strategy.

3. Review and assess the leadership roles in the organization in order to determine where to focus leadership-development efforts.

4. Integrate succession planning with your recruiting, orientation, development, appraisal, and retirement processes.

SELF-COACHING QUESTIONS

1. What are my organization's leadership needs?
2. How effective is our succession-planning process?

3. How well does our succession-planning process integrate with our recruiting, orientation, development, appraisal, and retirement processes?

4. What gaps and opportunities exist regarding succession planning in our organization?

5. What steps can I take to improve succession planning in our organization?

INSIGHT #38

Making Rank
Moving Up in Your Career

FEW TOPICS capture people's attention more than how to be promoted.

Promotion can signify many things: the attainment of a career goal, a pay raise, enhanced prestige, more benefits and perks, additional responsibility, a competitive win over other promotable colleagues, reward for work performed, a vacation home or boat, or another step toward your own personal growth.

As you continue your leadership journey, promotion opportunities enable you to serve at higher levels of responsibility and achieve your personal and professional goals.

In the armed forces, because rank is so central to the military hierarchy, the system is built to incentivize, support, and push promotion. Assignments, training, schools, evaluations, decorations, boards, mentoring, and development teams are all used to help service men and women advance to higher levels of responsibility.

Most enlisted personnel and officers learn fairly quickly what it takes to be promoted, especially if they decide to make a career of military service. And therein lies the key: learn what it takes to get promoted in your organization, and then work diligently to accomplish those things.

During my Air Force career, it took me a while to figure things out—and figure myself out—before I understood what I needed to do to become competitive for promotion. Early on, my priorities were skewed. During my first few years, I was too concerned about having fun to be serious about my job. As I matured, I learned that, in order to put myself in the hunt for promotion, I had to compete well against my peers. As it turned out, I was competing against Olympic-caliber leaders who were extremely competent and just as competitive as I was.

To succeed in this intense arena, I did the following:

- Sought out the tough, high-risk jobs that no one wanted and worked my tail off to succeed
- Made sure to deliver results
- Went on deployments and did my part to support wartime operations
- Built a solid network of trusted friends and colleagues
- Continued my education and kept learning

My efforts resulted in a number of choice assignments, including five commands, early promotions, and what ended up being a very gratifying military career.

DEEPER INSIGHT

Some organizations, such as the military, value seniority, skills, and performance; others may value different criteria. Again, the key is to figure out the "what" that leads to promotion.

Once you know that, there are some best practices you can apply to assist you along the road to promotion (Asher, 2007). These include:

- **Do what you're good at.** Playing to your strengths is always the wise move. Not only does the work leverage what you know best, but if you work for the right company, the path to promotion is paved more smoothly for you.

- **Do what you love to do.** If you are doing what you are good at and you love to do it, then "work" becomes "joy." This is the ultimate sweet spot that can facilitate a speedy rise up the corporate ladder.

- **Work for the right company.** Be sure the company you work for, core business, culture, and values align with your personality, strengths, skills, preferred working style, and values. There is such a thing as company-employee fit.

- **Find the right boss(es).** If you have the choice, choose a boss you would enjoy working with and for. Ask yourself if you respect this person, if he is friendly and supportive, and if you can talk to him candidly. Perhaps most important is to ask yourself if he is someone you can trust and who will advocate for you.

- **Have a good attitude.** Be supportive of your company and those you work with. Smile and be positive. For some, this is difficult, but no one likes to hang around with (or promote) a gloomy Gus.

- **Get along with people.** Interpersonal skills and emotional intelligence often make or break a promotion.

- **Be a team player.** Do your part, support your colleagues, be someone they can count on in thick or thin. Never be the one who initiates or propagates gossip, and never backstab.

- **Develop yourself.** Strive to become even better at what you do, continually train and educate yourself, and seek stretch assignments. If your company has a formal development program, apply for it, or participate in it. Find a mentor and a coach to help you grow.
- **Map out a career plan and aspirations.** Know where you want to go, why, and how to get there.
- **Make the case for promotion.** Do this by your work ethic, your performance, and your attitude. And ask for promotion when the time is right.

★ ★ ★

Moving ahead in your career is part of the leadership journey. It affords you the opportunity to make a larger impact and touch more lives. But you have to earn it, not just by being expert in your job but also by demonstrating the broad range of expertise, maturity, and competence that adds huge value to the organization.

RECAP

1. Getting promoted is a central component of your leadership journey.
2. Be sure to understand the deeper reasons behind your desire for promotion.
3. Learn what your organization's promotion expectations are; then meet and exceed those expectations.
4. Apply the ten promotion best practices to orient your efforts toward your promotion goals.

SELF-COACHING QUESTIONS

1. What are my near-term and long-term promotion goals?
2. What are my deeper reasons for wanting to be promoted?

3. What does my organization expect from me in order to move me up the ladder?

4. What is my plan to meet those expectations?

5. Whom can I reach out to and rely on to help me get promoted?

INSIGHT #39

Achieving Warrior Resilience
Develop Your Internal Reserves

I ENTERED ACTIVE DUTY in October 1989 when Operation Desert Shield started, and for the next twenty-four years, the US Air Force was flying and fighting somewhere. So, for my entire career, I was associated with some sort of armed conflict, including the years following the tragic events of September 11, 2001.

Many soldiers, sailors, airmen, and marines with multiple deployments into combat zones have paid a very high price. Some have paid with their lives; many others continue to live with the aftereffects including post-traumatic stress disorder. As a result of that experience, the word *resilience*—being able to withstand and overcome extended stress—entered the military lexicon. In today's high-pressure, competitive business climate, private-sector leaders need resilience as well.

DEEPER INSIGHT

If you are a leader, especially at the executive level, you will experience higher levels of stress on the job than most. In fact, it will come continuously, sometimes in big doses. There are going to be times when the stress you are experiencing is out of your control, whether externally or internally driven. It is during such times that you need stress resilience to get you through. Lack of stress resilience leads to a reduction in performance due to decreases in cognitive intelligence, emotional intelligence, and physical and emotional health. In short, chronic stress is a real danger to you as a leader. Therefore, you must become stress resilient in order to deal with the demands of your role.

According to Dr. Henry Thompson (2010), author of *The Stress Effect,* when your stress-management capacity, cognitive resilience, and stress-resilient emotional intelligence are working together, you have the ability and reserves to productively manage stress.

Let's look at each of these factors.

Stress Management Capacity (SMC): According to Thompson, SMC is the "total ability the leader has to manage stress." Every leader has a finite SMC capacity or comfort zone. Go a little above the comfort zone, and you begin to experience burnout. Go a little below, and rust-out comes into play.

Burnout occurs while you are in periods of high stress. Although peak performance lies in the burnout zone, you will not be able to maintain this level for very long. I bet you've known leaders over the course of your career who look like a heart attack waiting to happen. You can literally see the stress coming off them.

In contrast, rust-out results from low-stress situations. While low stress might sound appealing, experiencing it for an extended period of time is not good for you. Staying too long in the rust-out zone leads to boredom, loss of purpose, and low motivation. Some studies show the health effects of rust-out are even more harmful than those of burnout. Working too long in the burnout and rust-out zones will have a negative impact on your cognitive abilities, emotional performance, decision making, and health.

Improving your SMC involves the systematic effort to push the envelope of your comfort zone in order to expand your upper and lower stress boundaries. Influencing factors include:

- **Meaning**—having a higher purpose for your life
- **Commitment**—pledging to do your best
- **Control**—your ability to mitigate stress
- **Motivation**—drive to take action to deal with stress
- **Awareness**—knowing when you are under stress
- **Reality**—looking your situation squarely in the eye
- **Sensitivity**—keeping stress in perspective
- **Coping**—implementing stress-reduction techniques

Your mind and body will attempt to maintain your current boundaries. The best approach is to work on it bit by bit, attacking the smaller stress-inducers first. Also, in order to stretch your stress boundaries, push just beyond your transition areas between the comfort zone and burnout and rust-out zones. Working in those transition areas is most conducive to expanding your SMC.

Cognitive Resilience (CR): Cognitive resilience ensures that the effects of stress do not adversely affect your memory, your ability to process information, the speed at which you process that information, and your facility for reasoning clearly. Focusing on your CR is a way to protect and increase your cognitive functioning while you are under stress.

Signs of loss in cognitive functioning include forgetting details; slowing down to take in information; asking for information to be repeated; or having trouble with analysis, reasoning, and calculations.

Thompson advocates that you visualize a "cognitive functioning dashboard" in order to increase awareness of your cognitive state and whether or not your performance is dropping. The components of the dashboard include your memory, ability to retrieve information, and reasoning sharpness.

One of the key enemies of CR is lack of sleep, especially chronic sleep loss. It's really important to know how much sleep you need and then to fight to get that amount each week. Short naps can be a huge help in closing your sleep deficit.

Another idea is to use performance aids. For example, if you don't absolutely have to remember something, don't. Use a reference or checklists to help out. This not only includes Google but also your employees. Strive to offload the extraneous cognitive tasks that take away from your CR.

Making decisions in advance is another way to sustain your CR. An example of this is establishing and rehearsing an emergency plan in case of a tornado or other natural disaster.

Stress-Resilient Emotional Intelligence (SREI): If you have stress-resilient emotional intelligence, Thompson says you possess "the ability to resist the negative influences of stress on the emotional aspects of decision making by flexing and adapting to sudden change."

When stress levels go up, a leader's ability to act in an emotionally intelligent way goes down, sometimes catastrophically. If you aren't emotionally intelligent (able to express and control your emotions, as well as to understand, interpret, and respond to the emotions of others), you begin to miss important information coming from your own emotions, compromise your ability to accurately assess the emotions of others, or fail to act in an emotionally appropriate way. So, not only does cognitive intelligence go down under stress, so does emotional intelligence. This is a negatively reinforcing spiral you want to avoid.

As with all components of stress resilience, it's important to be aware when your emotional intelligence is profoundly affected by stress. Your emotional intelligence dashboard reveals your energy level, mood, and emotional control. Decreases in these areas are indicators that something may be going on that is adversely affecting your emotional intelligence.

Increased emotional intensity, flying off the handle, putting off decisions, avoiding difficult conversations (or eagerly seeking them out) are all warning indicators. Also be aware of bodily indicators such as increases in heart rate and breathing, sweating, redness and blotching, twitching, and hot spots. Another technique is simply to ask yourself how you feel. Bringing your emotions into consciousness is a great way to step back and regain perspective.

Getting the proper amount of sleep does wonders for emotional intelligence. You might have noticed that, when you are sleep deprived, it is not only much harder to keep your emotions in check, you are also much less aware of emotional cues from others.

★ ★ ★

When your stress management capacity, cognitive resilience, and stress-resilient emotional intelligence are working together, you have both the capacity and reserves to productively manage stress. In unison, these three aspects of stress resilience ensure that you are able to withstand the stress of leadership and avoid a catastrophic leadership failure.

RECAP

1. As a leader, you will experience stress—at times, significant levels of stress.
2. In order to cope with stress, you need to put in place habits and behaviors that increase your resilience.

3. Continual stress negatively affects your ability to lead.

4. Three ways to build your stress resilience include increasing your stress-management capacity, raising your cognitive resilience, and improving your stress-resilient emotional intelligence.

SELF-COACHING QUESTIONS

1. How much stress do I experience on a regular basis?

2. How well am I dealing with the stresses of leadership?

3. What stress-resilience practices do I have in place to help me cope with stress?

4. What techniques can I practice to enhance my stress resilience?

INSIGHT #40

Get Your PT In
Take Care of Yourself

PHYSICAL TRAINING (PT) is part of being in the military. PT is necessary to withstand the demands of training exercises, deployments, battlefield conditions, and the relentless pace that comes with all of them.

As an airman, I was required to stay fit. I'm glad I did because this greatly enhanced my ability to deal with the day-to-day stresses of active duty, including deployments and command.

Early in my career, I fell back on my experience as a competitive runner to stay in shape. There was nothing I liked more than getting in a hard road run. However, I can't say that my nutrition was all that great. I ate most anything I wanted—and a lot of it. I never really had any problem getting enough sleep. The hard part for me was getting up in the morning.

Toward the end of my career, the toll of years of running forced me to diversify my exercise program. I incorporated speed walking, high-intensity exercise, hiking, biking, skiing, and even some rock climbing. I found that I enjoyed the variety and was able to stay in good shape. I had to make adjustments in my eating habits, too. No longer could I vacuum up anything that looked good to eat. It became important to make better food choices and watch my portion sizes. I also found that getting enough sleep and time away from the job became much more critical as the demands of my assignments increased.

I learned that this trio of exercise, good nutrition, and plenty of rest was a powerful elixir. The regimen kept my spiritual, psychological, and physical reserves up so that I could be the very best I could be every day.

DEEPER INSIGHT

The health benefits of exercise are well documented, but the benefits of exercise on your ability to deal with stress are equally important. Exercise increases blood flow to the brain and elevates your ability to combat the cognitive and emotional effects of stress.

Here are some things to do to get yourself out the door to exercise:

- Get a physical, preferably every year.
- Stop making excuses, get off your backside, and step out!
- Track your baseline measurements such as heart rate, blood pressure, and maximum oxygen uptake capability.
- Find out what form of exercise motivates you most: individual or group, indoor or outdoor, competitive or getting in the zone.
- Map out a schedule, and stick to it.
- Set reasonable goals. It's going to take time to progress, so enjoy the journey!

Eating right is fundamental to stress resilience. Your body depends on a strong, healthy flow of energy to manage stress. But this is easier said than done, especially in the United States. What tastes good and is readily available is not necessarily a healthy choice. So good nutrition requires discipline and time to form new habits.

Here are nine things you need to do to improve your nutrition:

- Make healthy food choices.
- Keep a food journal. It might surprise you to see what you put into your body. A journal is also a good way to stay focused on your eating plan.
- Weigh yourself each day, and record your weight.
- To change your eating habits, make small daily changes.
- Avoid fad diets.
- Don't eat junk food.
- Drink plenty of water every day.
- Cut back on or eliminate soft drinks.
- Control the size of your portions.

As I said earlier, getting sufficient rest is absolutely critical to your ability to cope with stress. You need rest to allow your brain and your body to regenerate and repair itself. Do your utmost to avoid losing sleep. Sleep loss is cumulative; your cognitive abilities, in particular, will suffer the longer you deprive yourself of adequate sleep.

Getting proper rest includes:

- Taking breaks during the day and sleeping at least eight hours a night.
- Taking time for yourself throughout the day to get away from the grind for short periods of time.
- Taking vacations, trips, and getaways.
- Saying no when you have to so that you resist overloading yourself unnecessarily.

- Identifying ways to rest and unwind from a hectic schedule such as walking, listening to music, meditation or relaxation exercises, a quick scan of the Web, or a short personal conversation with a colleague.

If you are like most Americans, you probably drink a lot of caffeinated drinks to keep going. Although studies have shown that caffeine can help boost performance, a caffeine jolt only works if you aren't consuming a lot of it in the first place.

Try to disengage from the day-to-day grind, and give yourself time away from the stress-inducing aspects of your job. This should include more than just a long weekend or a day off here or there. Take extended vacations that allow your body, mind, and spirit to recuperate.

★ ★ ★

Here is why all this is important: There are going to be times when the stress you are experiencing is out of your control. It could be externally driven or internally driven. During such times, you will need to draw on your stress-resilience habits, including regular PT, good nutrition, and rest to get you through.

RECAP
1. Proper exercise, nutrition, and sleep are essential to your ability to cope with the stresses of leadership.
2. Set up and stick with an exercise plan to increase your physical reserves during times of stress.
3. Think about what you eat; avoid junk food and fad diets.
4. Get plenty of sleep, and take time away to recharge.

SELF-COACHING QUESTIONS

1. How much exercise am I getting on a regular basis?
2. How committed am I to staying fit? What is my exercise plan?
3. What kind of food do I eat?
4. How conducive are my eating habits to good health?
5. How much sleep do I get as a rule? It is enough? How many hours do I need to be at my best?
6. Do I get tired in the middle of the day?
7. When was the last time I took a vacation?
8. What can I do to improve my exercise, eating, and rest habits?

INSIGHT #41

Be Family Strong
Take Care of Your Family

ALL TOO OFTEN, leaders end up working long, extended hours to deal with everything that comes at them in their positions. The pressure to perform and deliver results only adds to the temptation to do more and work harder and longer. The end result is that your family is neglected, and that's not good for anyone—not you, as a spouse and parent, and especially not for your kids.

I once worked for a boss who was as ambitious as they come. He was well known for keeping a frenetic pace from 0530 in the morning to well into the evening. I remember talking to his wife once. She mentioned that she never got to talk to him because when he got home, he collapsed on the recliner and fell asleep. What was even tougher to see was his (lack of) relationship with his kids. He was never there to create a relationship in the first place, much less nurture it.

Even worse, I heard a story of a very senior leader who told a group of young officers, "If you're not divorced or moving that way, you're not working hard enough." This was from a guy who followed his own advice.

I'm here to tell you that this is nothing to be proud of. It fact, it's downright shameful.

Part of the responsibility of heroic leaders is to be a model for others to emulate. Who wants to emulate, much less follow, leaders like these?

DEEPER INSIGHT

Never let your ambitions or duties get so overwhelming that they get in the way of what matters most—your family. If that means you have to schedule time to be with them, then do it.

I get it. Sometimes, the pressures and demands of leadership will make it very difficult to spend time with your family. But I caution you: Don't make succumbing to those demands a habit. Keep your priorities straight.

In *Life Matters: Creating a Dynamic Balance of Work, Family, Time, & Money*, Roger and Rebecca Merrill (2004) offer concrete ideas on how to strengthen your family and optimize the time you spend with them. First and foremost, they emphasize the concept of family leadership in terms of four basic parental roles:

- Provide the necessities of physical, social, emotional, and spiritual life.
- Protect family members from harm.
- Nurture family members with love and kindness.
- Teach family members principles and values that empower them to have rich, rewarding relationships and joyful, fulfilling lives.

With this foundation of family leadership in place, they recommend the following "optimizers" to strengthen your family life:

- Create a family mission statement. As a family, establish who you want to be and what is most important to all of you.

- Have weekly family time. Use this time to talk and have fun together.

- Have a "date night" with your spouse. Yes, going out for dinner and a movie together still works, even after many years of marriage.

- Share one-on-one time with your children both at home and outside the house.

- Hold regular parent chats. Keep the lines of communication open by asking questions such as, "What are you working on?" and "What can we do to help?"

- Have daily family wisdom time. Discuss the great thoughts, ideas, and people throughout history.

- Establish clear responsibilities for all family members. Along with this, create a system of open accountability.

In addition to these optimizers, you will find others that work for your family situation.

★ ★ ★

Make a sincere effort to do your level best as a partner and a parent to optimize your precious time to be with your family. Your investment in these most important relationships will create a reservoir of trust and love—real family strength—that will carry you through tough professional and personal times.

RECAP

1. As important as work is, your family is even more important.

2. To the extent that your ambition overshadows your commitment to your family, your family will suffer.

3. Keep your priorities straight, and put your family at the top of the list.

4. Make a sincere effort to take care of your family. Be honest with yourself and them about the pressures of your job; then make it a point to carve out family time.

5. Don't just go through the motions. Make the time you spend with your family count.

SELF-COACHING QUESTIONS

1. How committed am I to my family?

2. How do I show it?

3. What are my real priorities, and where does my family fit?

4. How do my work responsibilities affect my ability to spend time with my family?

5. What can I do to strengthen my family life?

INSIGHT #42

We Appreciate You
Serve Your Community

LEADERSHIP requires an ethic of service to your organization, your people, your family, and your community.

Throughout my military career, I made a point of getting involved with various projects that helped serve the community, such as Habitat for Humanity, food drives, elementary school events, and visits to orphanages. As I assumed increased levels of responsibility, I found that I was interacting with other community leaders to tackle issues of mutual concern. I was always grateful for the goodwill and cooperation we enjoyed.

At one base, a vexing issue emerged that involved the sale and use of "spice" and other synthetic drugs. Both military personnel and civilians were falling victim to these insidious substances.

Through investigating ways to deal with the problem, we quickly discovered that we needed the help of local government and law enforcement, as well as state government. Our goals were to raise awareness of the substances and their effects, place pressure on establishments that sold them, and implement ordinances and laws that prevented their sale and distribution.

In an amazingly short amount of time, local law enforcement increased surveillance of offending businesses; all twelve municipalities surrounding the base passed ordinances outlawing the sale of synthetic drugs; and the state legislature passed a law prohibiting the manufacturing, sale, and distribution of such substances. These actions, coupled with a series of measures we took on base, knocked the use of these particular drugs way down.

It was a proud moment for all of us that would never have been possible without cooperation among all affected groups in the community and those of us on base.

DEEPER INSIGHT

You can gain this type of support only by participating in the community in a helpful and positive way. It takes more than a sense of obligation to "be a good neighbor." Contributing to the community is a concrete way of extending your commitment to service and demonstrating to people outside your normal sphere of influence that they matter.

Well-conceived, well-implemented community involvement can help to:

- Enhance your organization's reputation as a good corporate citizen
- Address community needs
- Live your organization's core values
- Address stakeholder requirements and concerns
- Meet organizational legal obligations
- Enhance your overall strategy
- Build employee skills

Seek to be a "neighbor of choice" (Burke, 1999). You can do this by building relationships with key community leaders and organizations. Back up these relationships by anticipating and responding to the community's expectations and concerns. Be sure to structure your organization's community-outreach programs to both enhance the community's quality of life and support your organization's strategic goals.

★ ★ ★

Serving your community generates returns in terms of your organization's reputation and the goodwill of the community. And as a result of your community involvement, you will be more likely to get the support you need from the community, especially when you need it most.

RECAP

1. Seek to participate in and give back to your community.
2. Be a "neighbor of choice" by building relationships in your community and engaging in important initiatives and issues.
3. Align your community involvement with your organization's strategic goals.

SELF-COACHING QUESTIONS

1. How engaged am I with the community?
2. What is my community-engagement plan?
3. What community needs, issues, concerns, and expectations can my organization support and assist?
4. How can I personally contribute to the community in a positive and supportive way?

INSIGHT #43

Setting the Conditions for Your People to Perform
Your Role in Motivation

AFTER I RECEIVED MY COMMISSION as an officer in the US Air Force, I was required to serve for four years in return for the scholarship I had been given to pay for my college tuition. At the time, I was very motivated to be an officer and to embark on my first assignment. However, I was much less motivated to make the Air Force a career. After I had put in my four years, I submitted my paperwork to leave the service. My plan was to go to graduate school.

But before I transitioned out, my commander, a crusty old colonel named Skip Hardenburg, gave me the responsibility of bringing a new mission into our unit.

I thought, "OK, I have three months before I get out. I'll go ahead and do my part to set up the mission for success."

As I got into the job, a funny thing happened: I enjoyed it—loved it, in fact. It was new, challenging, demanding; I felt I was making a real contribution to our unit's success. A few weeks into the job, I went over to the base personnel office and pulled my separation paperwork. Instead of going to grad school, I decided I would spend a few more years in the Air Force. It turned out to be twenty more years.

In short, I became motivated to do my part for the mission and serve my county in a way that I had not considered before. Although it took a seasoned commander to see my potential and to create the right conditions, the motivation arose internally. I chose to act, to put forth effort, and to dedicate time to the mission and to the Air Force, which are the constituent elements of motivation.

Motivation is an indispensable part of leadership. And because you have a great deal of control over the work environment and conditions, you can help your people tap into their own motivation. That's what Colonel Skip Hardenburg did for me.

DEEPER INSIGHT

Although the way you fulfill your role as a motivator is very much an art, findings from more than eighty years of formal research on motivation provide a great deal of science you can draw on. Familiarizing yourself with these findings will help you better understand what you can do to enhance the motivational climate in which you operate.

Let's take a closer look at seven of the most important findings from motivation research.

- Needs can be physiological, psychological, or spiritual. Your most basic needs affect your survival and well-being. Satisfying these needs produces pleasurable feelings; having them frustrated or unmet feels painful or at least uncomfortable. But it can also be life-threatening (e.g., an unmet need for nourishment resulting in starvation). According to Abraham Maslow (1943), a pioneer in this field of study, needs are front and center when it comes to motivation. Understanding your people's needs can help you understand what motivates them, which then allows you to create conditions to satisfy their needs. Doing so enhances the goals and health of the organization.

- Job characteristics matter. Research over the years, such as that by Herzberg and his colleagues (1993) and by Hackman and Oldham (1980), has established that task variety, autonomy, recognition, opportunities to increase skills, and feedback all serve to motivate people. Motivation drops when any of these are diminished or missing. It is important to build these factors into job descriptions and to refer to them during your hiring, job development, and personal-development processes.

- The value you place on a goal or outcome and whether you expect to achieve it affects your motivation. For instance, you may place high value on winning the lottery, but you may not expect it to happen. So, this could lower your motivation to buy a ticket. Or, perhaps an employee comes to work early and stays late, expecting that this behavior will lead to a promotion down the road. If all that work doesn't result in a promotion, there's a good chance that employee's motivation will go down.

- Organizational justice—fairness and trust in the workplace—counts. When individuals believe they are being treated fairly, they tend to exhibit better job performance and engage in fewer conflicts and counterproductive activities. Motivation falls when a person thinks that a colleague is getting a better deal than she is, when processes seem biased against a particular individual or group, or when leadership is perceived as being unfair. Given the relationship between motivation and organizational justice, it is a leader's responsibility to ensure not only that it is practiced but also that it is observed and believed.

- The beliefs you have about your abilities (self-efficacy) have a direct impact on your success. The stronger your belief in yourself, the more likely you are to be successful. People with high self-efficacy are more likely to willingly take on difficult tasks, work harder to overcome tough challenges, and persist in seeing them through.

- Setting goals works. Performance goes up when people set goals, especially specific goals that are hard to reach but achievable. When a team commits to goals that are linked to outcomes it values, the resulting performance is even better. Well-constructed goals focus attention, energize effort, and inspire persistence in trying to reach the goal.

- Finding out what your people are thinking is an indispensable way to diagnose the good, the bad, and the ugly going on in your organization. There is a plethora of excellent employee-attitude surveys available to help you understand at a deeper level what is going on in your people's minds, which, in turn, can help you improve your organization's motivational environment. There is a simpler way, of course. If you want to know what people are thinking, ask them. Just walk around. Talk to them. In all likelihood, you'll find out plenty.

★ ★ ★

A leader's job is to bring people together to achieve common goals. Leadership is thus fundamentally linked to motivation. The seven principles of motivation presented here have been proven to bolster the motivational environment of many organizations. Use them to set the conditions for your people to perform—and succeed.

RECAP

1. Creating a positive motivational climate is among your most important responsibilities as a leader.

2. Motivation arises internally and is supported by external factors.

3. Eighty years of research on motivation have validated several principles on fostering motivation in employees.

4. Ultimately, the key is to understand your people's needs and seek to set up an environment in which those needs can more easily be met.

SELF-COACHING QUESTIONS

1. How familiar am I with my people's physiological, psychological, and spiritual needs?

2. What are some ways I can get to know my people better?

3. How would I assess the motivational climate in my organization?

4. What am I doing to create an environment that is conducive to building and sustaining a motivated workforce?

INSIGHT #44

Acknowledge Success
Celebrate Your Victories Large and Small

IN THE MIDST OF THE DAY-TO-DAY GRIND, it's easy to pass over or forget to celebrate progress. The victories you have, whether large or small, are the product of hard work and determination. And you and your team need to take time to congratulate yourselves.

During my last assignment in the Air Force as the commander of a worldwide deployable combat-communications unit, we were subjected to multiple readiness inspections. Preparation for these extremely thorough inspections required the dedicated efforts of all the airmen in the organization. No detail, no matter how insignificant, could be overlooked.

It so happened that one division of the unit, a squadron responsible for establishing communications and computer networking capability in austere environments, achieved a perfect score on an inspection. What was so special about this squadron's performance is that a perfect score had never before been awarded. This was the first and only squadron to do it. To say I was thrilled with their performance is an understatement.

The typical way for a commander to congratulate people on a job well done is to get the airmen in a formation, say some nice words, shake a few hands, and give out challenge coins (specially struck coins given to airmen for exemplary performance). But the result this squadron had achieved deserved something more.

I asked my staff to set up the obligatory formation, which they did. One chilly fall morning, I arrived at the squadron formation, climbed up on the back of a two-ton truck, and proceeded to say some nice words to all the airmen assembled. I told them that their performance was unprecedented, that they were the first, that they were champions, and that I was proud of them.

I told them that I was so proud of them that I wanted to celebrate with them. With that, I climbed off on the truck, walked into the middle of the formation, and asked them to gather around.

By this time, the airmen were buzzing: "What's he doing?" "What's going on?" "Colonels don't do things like this!"

At a nod of my head, one of my staff cranked the volume on the loudspeakers, and the opening bars of the "Harlem Shake" began to play. At this point, they all knew what was happening. People began to smile and laugh, especially when I began to do the dance with great gusto. Let me tell you, you've never lived until you've done the Harlem Shake with 150 of America's best sons and daughters.

What the airmen found even funnier is that as the song began to end, I was so into it, that I was the only one still dancing. They loved it, and so did I.

I wrapped up our celebration by giving the entire squadron a three-day pass—a prized reward.

For months afterward, airmen in that squadron came up to me to tell me how great it was that their colonel came out and did the Harlem Shake with them. It was a special moment for a special group of airmen, and I was happy to celebrate their accomplishment with them. And I bet somewhere, someone has a video of me doing the Harlem Shake.

DEEPER INSIGHT

It's vital for your morale and the morale of your team to take the time to celebrate, or at least acknowledge, the good things that your organization and your people do. Human beings need to know that what they're doing is worthwhile. We're not machines without emotions and spirits.

It's easy to get trapped in our daily routines, pursuing the completion of tasks and rushing to meet deadlines, without taking the time to pat ourselves and others on the back for a job well done. Such an approach causes any potential joy we might experience in our work lives to escape into the surrounding atmosphere and progressively drags our spirits down.

It's important for you to set aside time to tell your team "they done good." This message can be communicated in myriad ways from a simple smile and a thank you to an informal recognition ceremony to time off or a full-blown party.

★ ★ ★

Celebrate your victories large and small. You need it, and your people need it to revitalize and recharge your psychological, emotional, and spiritual batteries.

RECAP

1. Take the time to celebrate accomplishments.
2. Doing so will help you recharge your psychological, emotional, and spiritual batteries.
3. Be creative about planning your celebration.

SELF-COACHING QUESTIONS

1. How much fun are you having at work?

2. How much fun do you think your people are having?

3. When is the last time you celebrated a good result or great performance, either of your team or one of your people?

4. What are some ways that you can celebrate your victories?

INSIGHT #45

Bestowing Medals and Awards
Show Your People You Love Them

IN THE MILITARY, medals are given out as a mark of distinction for heroism, meritorious or outstanding service, or achievement. Medals are a key way to recognize military members for what they do, which by definition, involves risking life and limb. They are formal acknowledgments of how much leaders appreciate and value their people. But recognition doesn't always have to be formal.

During my second squadron command, I started a special commander's award program called the "cream-of-the-crop award." The award was an empty can of creamed corn mounted on a wooden pedestal with the simple inscription: "Presented by the Commander for Excellence—You are the Cream of the Crop." Sure, it was corny. But for me, it was a personal way to thank those hardworking members of the squadron who ordinarily were not lauded with more formal recognition.

After a while, the award became highly coveted, and it also worked well as a pen and pencil holder. People still say to me, years later, "Hey, sir, I still have that can of corn you gave me on my desk." That's pretty cool to hear.

DEEPER INSIGHT

The best leaders go out of their way to set up programs and processes to informally and formally recognize their people. Whether it's an employee-of-the-month program, an award that recognizes superior contributions over a period of time, or an empty can of corn, telling your people how much you appreciate them and what a great job they are doing goes a long way toward establishing loyalty, fostering self-esteem, creating inclusion, and bolstering retention.

As you seek to recognize your people, keep the following guidelines in mind (based on Deeprose, 1994):

- Be fair.
- Specify reward criteria, whether informal or formal.
- Reward those who meet the criteria.
- Take the time to say thank you—often.
- Recognize teams as well as high-performing individuals.
- Align recognition with your people's intrinsic motivational needs.
- Recognize and reward what you expect in terms of behavior and outcomes.

★ ★ ★

Although research has shown that the effects of external motivation rarely last because motivation comes from within, I know few people who don't like to be told "good job" or "thank you." This is what recognition is really all about: that personal touch that tells people you value them.

RECAP

1. Recognize your people for the hard work they do.
2. Recognition doesn't have to always be formal. A simple thank you can go a long way.
3. Although the external motivation provided by recognition rarely lasts, the most important point is to make it sincere and personal.

SELF-COACHING QUESTIONS

1. How often do I recognize my people, formally or informally?
2. How often do I thank them?
3. How fair is our formal recognition program?
4. What are some specific ways in which I can recognize my people?

DEEPER INSIGHT

Humility means having authentic pride in yourself, your achievements, and your gifts—without being egotistical. It is the opposite of hubris—the arrogance that clouds judgment and distorts reality to the point of a failure in leadership.

Being humble means having a quiet confidence, letting others discover your talents without having to boast about them, and recognizing others for their gifts and talents, no matter what their station. It also means that you're OK with not having all the answers and understand that you may make mistakes from time to time.

Humility also involves empathy and the ability to accurately perceive and attend to the needs of the organization and its people, especially those who work for you. According to Professor Harry Kraemer (2011), genuine humility allows leaders to be authentic and thus live out their personal values, while respecting the values of those around them: "At the heart of genuine humility is never forgetting who you are, appreciating the value of each person in the organization, and treating everyone respectfully, whether she is a senior manager or a summer intern."

There's an old military saying: the higher you rise in rank, the smarter, funnier, and better looking you become. It's a warning against the temptations that great power brings. Even the most humble among us are vulnerable to the threat of misplaced pride and ego gratification.

However, it's not easy to cultivate humility, especially when our society seems to promote self-aggrandizing achievement and competition along with the adulation that comes with it. Being humble goes against conventional thinking and challenges our egos. But humility is an essential attribute of a leader.

As you work to achieve humility, keep these questions in mind:

- Do I seek the acknowledgment of others when I put myself out for them?

- Do I become envious or frustrated when others are recognized for their accomplishments?
- Do I recognize when I am acting overly self-serving or arrogant?
- How much do I compare myself to others?
- How likely am I to serve others?
- Do I boast about my accomplishments?
- Am I truly humble, and if so, how do I exhibit humility?

★ ★ ★

Humility is grounded in values-based self-awareness, a clear moral sense, and ethical behavior. It's a selfless orientation in the employment of one's gifts, talents, and skills in the service of others. Make humility the backbone of your leadership style.

RECAP

1. Humility is a foundational component of leadership.
2. Humility is externally oriented toward the welfare of others and your organization.
3. As the opposite of arrogance, humility allows you to keep your eyes open in a clear-eyed, realistic way.
4. Humility is a constituent component of an ethic of service.

SELF-COACHING QUESTIONS

1. Do I truly embody the spirit of humility as I interact with others in my organization?
2. How do others view me in terms of my humility?
3. What are some examples of humility I have witnessed in my professional life?
4. How can I learn to value others more than I value myself?

INSIGHT #47

Working for Napoleon
How to Deal with Negative Leadership

I'VE HAD MY SHARE of tough bosses, and I'm sure you have, too. I've been cussed at, thrown out of offices, publicly belittled, demeaned, ridiculed, ignored, yelled at, and threatened.

In all of these cases, I was not the only one being treated badly by these leaders. We were all the victims of a pattern of poor leadership behavior. The way those leaders acted was out of line, whether or not I had fallen short in my performance. For my part, I grew a thick skin partly in self-defense and partly to ensure that I could retain the inner resources I needed to do my job.

Some of these leaders received their just deserts: they were reassigned, demoted, forced to resign, or fired. Others continued to get promoted.

Sadly, bosses like these exist in workplace after workplace. They exhibit the full range of abusive, tyrannical, bullying, destructive, and toxic behavior. In so doing, they wreak havoc on the organizations they lead and the people who work for them.

DEEPER INSIGHT

Negative behavior on the part of a leader has deleterious effects on organizations and people, including lower job performance, poorer attitudes, decreased expectations of equity and justice, increased turnover and absenteeism, and less organizational commitment and citizenship behaviors (Tate, 2011).

Negative leaders can be abusive, tyrannical, destructive, bullying, or toxic.

- **Abusive leaders** display hostile verbal and nonverbal behaviors that do not include physical contact.
- **Tyrannical leaders** rule by fear and intimidation in order to gain and maintain control.
- **Destructive leaders** undermine, sabotage, and violate the interests of the organization—driving down member motivation, well-being, and job satisfaction.
- **Leaders who bully** use mental or physical strength to weaken, intimidate, embarrass, and control their people.
- **Toxic leaders** engage in willful destructive behaviors that undermine morale, motivation, self-esteem, and well-being; they usually exhibit dysfunctional personal characteristics (unbridled ambition, narcissism, lack of integrity, psychological imbalance).

None of these leadership types ends up doing much good for the organization or the people they lead. However, the fact remains that there's a good chance you'll work for one. So what can you do when you encounter a negative leader?

At a fundamental level, you must remember that the only person you can control is you. Once you realize this, you can help yourself immensely by analyzing your situation and selecting useful behaviors of your own to contain the relationship within tolerable bounds.

Dr. Roy Lubit (2003), author of *Coping with Toxic Managers, Subordinates ... and Other Difficult People*, offers some survival tactics for dealing with difficult leaders.

- **Narcissists:** Avoid criticizing them, show admiration, play down your accomplishments and talents, explain how your ideas fit into their plans.

- **Control freaks:** Avoid direct suggestions, let them think new ideas are their own, don't criticize them, show admiration and respect, don't outshine them, play down your accomplishments, document your work.

- **Antisocial:** Avoid provoking them, don't get dragged into their questionable activities, seek allies, find another position.

- **Ruthless:** Watch your back.

- **Bully:** Stay out of their way; don't let them intimidate you.

- **Frantic:** Help them with their objectives; help them set a more reasonable pace.

- **Irritable:** Find out what upsets them and avoid that, provide support, work with them to lessen the impact of their behavior.

- **Compulsive:** Work with them to explore different ways of accomplishing a task; avoid arguing about the best way to do it.

- **Authoritarian:** Work with them to introduce other ways of accomplishing a task in ways that people they respect accomplish it.

- **Oppositional:** Make them feel that they are a part of the decision.

- **Passive-aggressive:** Encourage their participation.

In all cases, it is vital that you establish a support network of friends, colleagues, and mentors who can help you keep your perspective, blow off steam, and evaluate options for dealing with the situations in which you find yourself. Always remember that you can choose to seek another position elsewhere.

★ ★ ★

Negative leaders are unfortunately a fact of life. Knowing how to deal with them is therefore an essential leadership skill you need for navigating rough seas.

RECAP

1. At some point in your career, you will work for a negative leader, so it's important to your survival and to your career that you become skilled in dealing with them.

2. While you won't be able to control negative leaders, by your considered interactions with them, you will increase your chances of containing their impact on you and your people.

3. Evaluate the negative leader carefully, and select behaviors and actions that help you have as productive a relationship as possible with him.

4. Call on your support network of friends, colleagues, and mentors. You may also want to hire a professional coach.

SELF-COACHING QUESTIONS

1. What does having a boss who is a negative leader cost me personally and professionally?

2. How does it affect my values and ability to live them?

3. What are my options?

4. How well can I tolerate the situation?

5. What is the likely outcome of this relationship?

6. How can I change the situation?

INSIGHT #48

What to Do When the Worst Occurs
Dealing with Tragedy

TRAGEDY COMES IN ALL FORMS, and dealing with its aftermath, which often involves loss, is never easy. Loss and grief are painful human experiences. But when tragedy occurs, your people will look to you for reassurance, hope, security, and strength as they work through the painful emotions that accompany such events.

At the beginning of this book, I mentioned two tragic events that affected my organization and me in a very personal way: a suicide and the disbanding of our unit. I resolved to lead through these events with honor, dignity, and professionalism. There was no manual to help me prepare for such occurrences or guide me through them when they occurred. However, I found that my experience and training were invaluable resources to draw on.

That said, there is a large body of research on crisis management and trauma response that could have proved very helpful as I worked my way through these very trying circumstances.

DEEPER INSIGHT

In your role as a leader, it is your responsibility to help your organization recover from tragedies. You must point the way forward, but you must take into consideration the emotions your people are experiencing so you know when your organization is ready to move on.

In the immediate aftermath of a tragedy, people can experience intense sadness; recurring images of the event; or withdrawal and avoidance of people, places, and things that remind them of the event. In addition, they will exhibit their emotions in different ways. Some may act them out, others may internalize them, and still others may delay even experiencing them.

In addition to providing a reassuring, strong leadership presence, your most important task is to communicate compassionately. You can do this by sharing grief, inspiring hope, providing facts, and managing rumors throughout the duration of the incident.

The way in which you respond will change depending on where you are in relation to the tragedy: in the midst of it, in the immediate aftermath, in the moving-ahead stage, or in recovery.

In the midst of the event

- Remain calm and in control of your emotions.
- If needed, set up a crisis-response team.
- Ensure that you are getting the best available information about the situation.
- Provide updates to the organization as you determine the facts.
- See to the safety and well-being of your people, especially those directly affected by the event.

Immediately after the event

- Be very visible and make frequent appearances and announcements.
- Provide accurate information, especially on what you know, don't know, and need to find out.

- Keep your messages as simple and as positive as you can.
- Use multiple avenues to get your messages out.
- Be calm and encouraging when you speak.

As the event evolves beyond the immediate aftermath
- Keep track of ongoing needs and resources such as health and public safety.
- Provide clear guidance and expectations to your support team, while also delegating appropriately.
- As applicable, ensure that memorial services are organized according to the wishes of involved families. Pay attention to the timing of these services.
- Be sure to attend these services, and remember that it's OK for you to show grief.

In the recovery phase
- Keep your focus on a common set of future goals.
- Thank all those who helped. Establish avenues for those who want to help to be able to do so.
- Avoid the blame game. Your job is to facilitate healing and reconstitute your organization so that your people are able to return to normalcy.
- Don't move too quickly or too slowly. Stay in touch with the emotional and psychological climate around you.
- Acknowledge and even celebrate progress.

★ ★ ★

Tragedies will take a toll on your inner reserves and stress resilience. Continue to listen to your advisers, seek input, and get feedback. Be sure you are taking care of yourself with proper rest, nutrition, and physical activity. Get the support you need from family, friends, colleagues, and medical and spiritual professionals.

RECAP

1. Leading through tragedy is one of the most difficult challenges of leadership.

2. You must provide a reassuring, strong, yet human leadership presence for your people.

3. The way in which you communicate with your people is vital in helping them deal with the event.

4. Ensure that you stay attuned to the emotional and psychological climate within your organization so that you can respond appropriately to needs as they arise.

5. Your response will change with each phase of the tragedy.

6. Be sure you take care of yourself throughout this period. Remember, you can't help others deal with stressful times if *you* are not in a condition to deal with them.

SELF-COACHING QUESTIONS

1. How prepared am I to lead through tragedy, grief, and loss in my organization?

2. How full is my stress-resilience bucket if a tragic event were to occur?

3. What can I do to increase my ability to lead through tragedy?

INSIGHT #49

Commanding the Room
Leading with Presence

HAVE YOU EVER BEEN AROUND A LEADER who could easily command a room or who appeared larger than life? What about a leader who made you feel instantly comfortable and listened to you as if you were the most important person in the world? Or one who spoke so honestly that you felt you knew what he was all about?

If so, you have an idea of what leadership presence is.

During my military career, I encountered many people who had some of these attributes but few who had all of them. Most often, the leaders I encountered had charisma—a kind of exterior magnetism and ability to move people emotionally.

But authentic leadership presence is more than just charisma.

DEEPER INSIGHT

According to leadership expert James Scouller (2011), presence is at its root inner wholeness—"the rare but attainable inner alignment of self-identity, purpose, and feelings that eventually leads to freedom from fear." Presence is what allows others to trust you and inspires them to want you as their leader.

Leaders with presence radiate an authenticity that pulls others toward them. Because these leaders no longer fear revealing their true nature, they are able to devote their full attention to others, speak honestly, and let their unique personalities flow.

There are eight elements that compose leadership presence: personal power, high self-esteem, a drive toward personal growth, a sense of purpose, concern and respect for others, intuition, living in the present, inner peace of mind, and a sense of fulfillment.

- **Personal power:** the ability to take responsibility for your choices and to exercise control of your psyche and your response to external events
- **High self-esteem:** a positive assessment of yourself, which frees you up to respect and admire others
- **A drive toward personal growth:** moving beyond limiting beliefs and mindsets that hold you back from achieving your full potential
- **A sense of purpose:** connecting to your core values and letting those values propel you to serve a cause bigger than you
- **Concern and respect for others:** a fundamental bias toward the welfare of your people
- **Intuition:** the ability to perceptively read situations and anticipate events
- **Living in the present:** being in the here and now rather than being diverted by memories, beliefs, and feelings of the past or overly fixated on hopes or fears about the future
- **A sense of peace and fulfillment:** a feeling that flows from all of the above elements—respecting yourself and knowing who you are and what you stand for

All of these qualities engender wholeness and being your genuine self, powerfully, wisely, fearlessly, and creatively.

★ ★ ★

The great thing is that presence can be developed—so that you, too, can radiate that elusive yet powerful quality of authentic leadership presence.

RECAP

1. Leadership presence arises from the inner alignment of self-identity, purpose, and feelings, as well as freedom from fear of revealing your true self.

2. Presence inspires people to trust you and want you as their leader.

3. There are eight elements of presence: personal power, high self-esteem, a drive toward personal growth, a sense of purpose, concern for and respect for others, intuition, living in the present, inner peace of mind, and a sense of fulfillment.

4. Leadership presence can be honed and developed.

SELF-COACHING QUESTIONS

1. Do I have leadership presence? Do others think I do?

2. How free am I from inner psychological division, fears, and limitations?

3. What is my self-concept? Who am I as a person?

4. How genuinely other-oriented am I?

5. What can I do to develop authentic leadership presence?

6. How willing am I to do the inner work required to build it?

INSIGHT #50

Keep Moving Forward
Commit to Reflection, Growth,
and Renewal as a Heroic Leader

LEADERSHIP IS a vastly complex endeavor, and therefore it's easy to oversimplify it into a checklist. Just follow the checklist, and call it good.

That's exactly what I DON'T want you to do with these insights.

Rather, what I'm asking you to do is to internally reflect on each of them to open your sight to their meaning for you. Thus, the word *insight*.

Becoming the leader you were called to be involves a lifetime process of continuous growth and renewal as you gain new and deeper insights, discard or modify old beliefs and practices, acquire new ones, and advance others.

This can occur only if you take the time to regularly step away from *doing* what it takes to lead to *being open* to the wisdom that can come only from reflection, growth, and renewal. Learning to become a better leader does not necessarily have to happen through the school of hard knocks.

Those still, quiet moments when you silently take time to tune into the organic process of growth in knowledge, understanding, and wisdom will recharge your spiritual batteries so that you are the best leader you can be. So use these fifty insights to energize your leadership development.

Reflection, growth, and renewal are critical elements of your personal leadership forge. From them flows everything on which your intrinsic power as a leader is built.

Time to Take Your Hero's Journey

NOW THAT YOU'VE READ THE FIFTY INSIGHTS, there are three important questions that lie before you.

Are you willing to step into the arena of heroic leadership with all of its joys, hardships, ups and downs, challenges, and opportunities?

As stated at the beginning of the book, the hero's journey is one in which you venture into a role that challenges your competency, skills, and psychological mettle on a daily basis. You are going to face complex problems that threaten the success of your strategy and the ongoing survival of your organization. You will stumble and even fail along the way.

Despite these tests of your leadership, will you have the self-awareness, fortitude, resilience, faith, and humility to drive on?

Your willingness to endure these crucibles will forge you into someone capable of producing a distinct and personal form of greatness. And great leaders are exactly what we need today.

Will you be one of them?

About the Author

JOE SCHERRER'S CAREER AS A LEADER was forged during twenty-four years as an officer in the US Air Force.

He is a highly decorated Air Force veteran and was deployed in support of seven overseas operations. He commanded five units at the wing, group, and squadron levels, completing his career as the commander of the Air Force's only combat-coded, deployable communications wing.

Joe's military background, particularly in the area of leading airmen, definitively shaped his personality and character. Throughout his career, his greatest passion was to see airmen succeed in their missions and their careers.

Joe earned a bachelor's degree in electrical engineering from Washington University in St. Louis and a master's degree in business administration from Boston University. He attended the Air Force Institute of Technology, the Naval War College, and the Air War College, earning a master's degree and distinguished graduate honors from each.

Joe is on the faculty of Washington University in St. Louis, where he teaches in the master of cyber security management program. He has published articles and papers on cyberspace operations, network-centric warfare, deployed communication, and command and control. He was the principal author and team leader for the first national military strategy for cyberspace operations. This policy document subsequently shaped the Department of Defense's response to the challenges and threats in that domain.

A popular and sought-after speaker, Joe is an experienced teacher of leadership skills and an expert in creating the total team effort required to fight and win on the battlefield, in the business arena, and in service organizations.

About The Leadership Crucible

THE MISSION OF THE LEADERSHIP CRUCIBLE is to inspire hope by forging leaders who work to make the world a better place.

At The Leadership Crucible, we teach executive leaders how to overcome their greatest challenges, produce results, achieve their goals, and become better leaders. Whether you are assuming new leadership responsibilities or are an established executive, we will help to make you the very best leader you can be.

The Leadership Crucible provides executive and career coaching, leadership seminars, leadership-development programs, customized leadership programs, and professional speaking that are tailored to individuals and organizations.

Our signature offering is *The Leadership Forge*, a holistic, six-step process based on military strategist John Boyd's work in classic military strategy, operational campaign planning, practical execution, and feedback at the tactical level—in the trenches, where real leadership happens.

The Leadership Forge builds a framework to guide our clients through an experience- and research-based leadership-development curriculum founded on time-tested military principles. The step-by-step framework consists of discovery, mission analysis, mission planning, deployment, intelligence assessment, and mission debrief.

The heart of The Leadership Forge approach is coaching leaders to produce and implement individualized campaign plans. These plans are built to effect change, drive results, and develop the participant's full potential as a leader.

TO CONTACT THE LEADERSHIP CRUCIBLE

To learn more about our services or to share your insights, thoughts, and comments about this book, please visit our website, theleadershipcrucible.com; e-mail joe@theleadershipcrucible.com; or call 636-209-3270.

Acknowledgments

IF YOU'RE DRIVING DOWN A COUNTRY ROAD, and you see a turtle on a fencepost, you know that turtle didn't get there by itself. It had some help.

Well, I'm that turtle, and I had a lot of help getting up on that fencepost as I wrote this book.

It has always been my dream to write a book, especially about one of my great passions—leadership. But it takes a team to succeed, and I was fortunate to have an outstanding group of people who supported me along this journey. Without them, this book would not have seen the light of day or passed quality muster.

- Dina Scherrer, my biggest cheerleader, whose constant belief in me made all the difference.

- Bobbi Linkemer, my editor, whose expertise transformed the book into something coherent and accessible.

- Peggy Nehmen, my book designer, who turned the idea of *The Leadership Forge* into a visual reality.

- Bonnie Spinola, my copyeditor, whose attention to detail improved the overall quality of the book.

- Donna Brodsky, whose proofreading added that last coat of showroom polish to the book.

- My reviewers: Dick Palmieri, Jim Neighbors, Innocent Nweze, Mickey Addison, Chuck Pugh, Sharyn McWhorter, Nicolette Wills, Michelle Russell, Kathy Ver Ecke, Antrese Wood, Tom Dorl, Doug Irwin, Sharon McInnis, and Doug Freund. Thank you for your feedback; you provided crucial perspective where I needed it most.

- I am also indebted to many amazing leaders I met throughout my Air Force career. It's due to their mentorship (and patience) that I learned to lead in my own right: Senior Master Sergeant Bob Koller, Colonel R. Keith Miller, Colonel Skip Hardenburg, Lieutenant General James Record, Brigadier General Gil Hawk, Colonel Bob Wright, Lieutenant General Bob Shea (USMC), Colonel Rob Gearhart (USMC), Brigadier General Jon Norman, Brigadier General Dave Cotton, Colonel Dave Kovach, Major General Dale Meyerrose, and Lieutenant General Andy Busch.

RECOMMENDED READING

Insight #1: Leadership Is a Hero's Journey
Start Yours Now

Campbell, J. A. (1949). *The hero with a thousand faces.* Princeton, NJ: Princeton University Press.

Cohen, W. A. (2010). *Heroic leadership: Leading with integrity and honor.* San Francisco: Jossey-Bass.

Congressional Medal of Honor Society: http://www.cmohs.org/

Insight #2: Get Clear on Your Leadership Sight Picture
How to Power Your Leadership by Knowing Who You Are and What You Stand For

MOTIVATORS

Reiss, S. (2000). *Who am I?: The 16 basic desires that motivate our actions and define our personalities.* New York: The Berkeley Publishing Group.

COGNITIVE INTELLIGENCE

Schmidt, F. L., & Hunter, J. E. (1998). The validity and utility of selection methods in personnel psychology: Practical and theoretical implications of 85 years of research findings. *Psychological Bulletin*, 124(2), 262.

EMOTIONAL INTELLIGENCE

Barling, J., Slater, F., & Kelloway, E. K. (2000). Transformational leadership and emotional intelligence: An exploratory study. *Leadership & Organization Development Journal*, 21(3), 157–161.

Goleman, D. (2011). *Leadership: The power of emotional intelligence.* Northampton, MA: More Than Sound.

Ruderman, M., Hannum, K., Leslie, J. B., & Steed, J. L. (2001). Making the connection: Leadership skills and emotional intelligence. *Leadership in Action*, 21(5), 3–7.

Stein, S., & Book, H. (2011). *The EQ edge: Emotional intelligence and your success.* Mississauga, ON: Jossey-Bass.

STRENGTHS

Peterson, C., & Seligman, M. (2004). *Character strengths and virtues: a handbook and classification.* Washington, DC/New York: American Psychological Association/Oxford University Press.

Snyder, C. R. (2010). *Positive psychology: The scientific and practical explorations of human strengths.* Thousand Oaks, CA: Sage Publications.

BLIND SPOTS

Blakeley, K. (2007). *Leadership blind spots—and what to do about them.* San Francisco: Jossey-Bass.

Hogan, J., Hogan, R., & Kaiser, R. B. (2010). Management derailment. In *American Psychological Association handbook of industrial and organizational psychology* (pp. 555–575), 3.

BIASES

Ariely, D. (2010). *Predictably irrational: The hidden forces that shape our decisions.* New York: Harper Perennial.

Kahneman, D. (2013). *Thinking, fast and slow.* New York: Farrar, Straus and Giroux.

DOMINANT PATTERNS

Charvet, S. (1997). *Words that change minds: Mastering the language of influence.* Dubuque, IA: Kendall/Hunt.

MORAL BELIEFS AND ETHICAL CODE

Johnson, C. (2009). *Meeting the ethical challenges of leadership: casting light or shadow.* Los Angeles: SAGE.

PASSIONS

Robinson, K., & Aronica, L. (2009). *The element: How finding your passion changes everything.* New York: Viking.

LIMITING DISTORTIONS

Burns, D. (1999). *Feeling good: The new mood therapy.* New York: Whole Care.

Scouller, J. (2011). *The three levels of leadership: How to develop your leadership presence, knowhow, and skill.* Cirencester, UK: Management Books 2000.

RESILIENCE

Thompson, H. (2010). *The stress effect: Why smart leaders make dumb decisions—and what to do about it.* San Francisco: Jossey-Bass.

HUMILITY

Collins, J. (2001). *Good to great: Why some companies make the leap—and others don't.* New York: HarperBusiness.

SERVICE

Greenleaf, R. (1977). *Servant leadership: A journey into the nature of legitimate power and greatness.* New York: Paulist Press.

Greenleaf, R., & Spears, L. (1998). *The power of servant-leadership: Essays.* San Francisco: Berrett-Koehler Publishers.

Insight #3: It's About "Duty, Honor, Country"
Lead with the Power of Your Values

Barrett, R. (2010). *The new leadership paradigm.* Asheville, NC: Barrett Values Center.

Burns, J. (2010). *Leadership.* New York: HarperPerennial.

Dean, K. (2008). *Values-based leadership: How our personal values impact the workplace.* The Journal of Values-Based Leadership, 1(1), 60–67.

Kovanic, N., & Johnson, K. D. (2005). *Lies and truths: Leadership ethics in the 21st century.* Terre Haute, IN: Rule of Thumb Publishing.

O'Toole, J. (1996). *Leading change: The argument for values-based leadership,* San Francisco: Jossey-Bass.

Peregrym, D. Values-based leadership: The foundation of transformational servant leadership. *The Journal of Values-Based Leadership,* 6(2).

Rokeach, M. (1973). *The nature of human values.* New York: The Free Press.

Rue, R. (2001). Values-based leadership: Determining our personal values. *Behavioral Science,* 30(4), 12–16.

Schwartz, S. H. (1992). Universals in the content and structure of values: Theory and empirical tests in 20 countries. In M. Zanna (Ed.), *Advances in experimental social psychology* (Vol. 25), pp. 1–65. New York: Academic Press.

Insight #4: Washington at Newburgh
Compromise Your Morals, Forfeit Your Right to Lead

Brown, M. E., & Treviño, L. K. (2006). Ethical leadership: A review and future directions. *The Leadership Quarterly,* 17(6), 595–616.

Mendonca, M. & Kanungo, R. (2007). *Ethical leadership.* Maidenhead, UK/New York: McGraw-Hill/Open University Press.

Thornton, T. (2006). Judgement and the role of the metaphysics of values in medical ethics. *Journal of Medical Ethics,* 32(6), 365–370.

Treviño, L. K., Brown, M., & Hartman, L. P. (2003). A qualitative investigation of perceived executive ethical leadership: Perceptions from inside and outside the executive suite. *Human Relations,* 56(1), 5–37.

Insight #5: Lead With Superpowers
Leverage Your Strengths

Buckingham, M., & Clifton, D. O. (2001). *Now, discover your strengths.* New York: Free Press.

Peterson, C., & Seligman, M. E. P. (2004). *Character strengths and virtues: A handbook and classification.* Washington, DC: American Psychological Association.

Rath, T., & Conchie, B. (2008). *Strengths based leadership: Great leaders, teams, and why people follow.* New York: Gallup Press.

Seligman, M. E. P. (2002). *Authentic happiness: Using the new positive psychology to realize your potential for lasting fulfillment.* New York: Free Press.

Zenger, J. H. (2012). *How to be exceptional: Drive leadership success by magnifying your strengths.* New York: McGraw-Hill.

Insight #6: Powell, Rumsfeld, or Wooden?
Base Your Leadership Success on a Great Model

Bass, B. M., & Avolio, B. J. (Eds.). (1994). *Improving organizational effectiveness through transformational leadership.* Thousand Oaks, CA: Sage Publications.

Burns, J. (2010). *Leadership.* New York: HarperPerennial.

Collins, J. (2001). *Good to great: Why some companies make the leap—and others don't.* New York: HarperBusiness.

Graen, G. B., & Uhl-Bien, M. (1995). Relationship-based approach to leadership: Development of leader-member exchange (LMX) theory of leadership over 25 years: Applying a multi-level multi-domain perspective. Special Issue: Leadership: The multiple-level approaches (Part 1). *Leadership Quarterly, 6,* 219–247.

Greenleaf, R. (1977). *Servant leadership: A journey into the nature of legitimate power and greatness.* New York: Paulist Press.

Greenleaf, R. K. (2008). *The servant as leader.* Westfield, IN: Greenleaf Center for Servant Leadership.

Peterson, C., & Seligman, M. (2004). *Character strengths and virtues: A handbook and classification.* Washington, DC/New York: American Psychological Association/Oxford University Press.

Scouller, J. (2011). *The three levels of leadership: How to develop your leadership presence, knowhow, and skill.* Cirencester, UK: Management Books 2000.

Yukl, G., & Lepsinger, R. (2004). *Flexible leadership: Creating value by balancing multiple challenges and choices.* San Francisco: Jossey-Bass.

Zenger, J., & Folkman, J. (2009). *The extraordinary leader: Turning good managers into great leaders.* New York: McGraw-Hill.

Insight #7: "I Do Solemnly Swear to Support and Defend"
Do You Pass the Buck or Accept the Blame?

Dive, B. (2008). *The accountable leader: Developing effective leadership through managerial accountability.* London/Philadelphia: Kogan Page.

Grimshaw, J., & Baron, G. (2010). *Leadership without excuses: How to create accountability and high performance (instead of just talking about it).* New York: McGraw-Hill Professional.

Ricks, T. (2012). *The generals: American military command from World War II to today.* New York: Penguin Press.

Insight #8: Of Generals and Admirals
Work Incessantly to Achieve Leadership Mastery

Brown, K. W., & Ryan, R. M. (2003). The benefits of being present: Mindfulness and its role in psychological well-being. *Journal of Personality and Social Psychology, 84* (4), 822–848.

Ericsson, K. (1996). *The road to excellence: The acquisition of expert performance in the arts and sciences, sports, and games.* Mahwah, NJ: Lawrence Erlbaum Associates.

Ericsson, K., Prietula, M., & Cokely, E. T. (2007). *The Making of an Expert by Harvard Business Review.* Cambridge, MA: Harvard Buisiness Review Press.

Gladwell, M. (2009). *Outliers: The story of success.* London: Penguin Books.

Greene, R. (2012). *Mastery.* New York: Viking.

Scouller, J. (2011). *The three levels of leadership: How to develop your leadership presence, knowhow, and skill.* Cirencester, UK: Management Books 2000.

Siegel, D. (2007). *The mindful brain: Reflection and attunement in the cultivation of well-being.* New York: W. W. Norton.

Insight #9: Win the War!
Create and Implement Your Campaign Strategy

Hrebiniak, L. (2005). *Making strategy work: Leading effective execution and change.* Upper Saddle River, NJ: Wharton School Pub.

Lafley, A., & Martin, R. L. (2013). *Playing to win: How strategy really works.* Boston: Harvard Business Review Press.

Press, H. B. S. (Ed.). (2005). *Strategy: Create and implement the best strategy for your business.* Boston: Harvard Business School Press.

von Clausewitz, K. (1832) *On war.*

Insight #10: Intelligence, Surveillance, and Reconnaissance
Sense the Competitive Environment

Boyd, J. R. (1976) "Destruction and Creation." US Army Command and General Staff College, September 3.

Coram, R. (2002). *Boyd: The fighter pilot who changed the art of war.* Boston: Little, Brown and Company.

Hammond, G. T. (2001). *The mind of war: John Boyd and American security.* Washington, DC: Smithsonian Books.

Osinga, F. P. (2006). *Science, strategy and war: The strategic theory of John Boyd.* New York: Routledge.

Richards, C. (2004). *Certain to win: The strategy of John Boyd, applied to business.* Philadelphia: Xlibris Corporation.

Insight #11: Stirrups, Airplanes, and Radios
You Must Deal With Change

Boyd, J. (1992). *A discourse on winning and losing.* Retrieved from http://www.ausairpower.net/APA-Boyd-Papers.html.

Kotter, J. P. (2012). *Leading change.* Boston: Harvard Business Review Press.

Liddell, H. B. H. (1999). *Thoughts on war.* Staplehurst, UK: Spellmount Publishers Ltd.

Insight #12: Power from the Edge
Leverage the Field for Innovation

Amabile, T. M. (1996). *Creativity and innovation in organizations* (Vol. 5). Boston: Harvard Business School.

Chang, S. C., & Lee, M. S. (2007). The effects of organizational culture and knowledge management mechanisms on organizational innovation: An empirical study in Taiwan. *The Business Review,* 7(1), 295–301.

Christensen, C., & Raynor, M. (2003). *The innovator's solution: Creating and sustaining successful growth.* Boston: Harvard Business School Press.

DeGraff, J. T., & Quinn, S. E. (2007). *Leading innovation: How to jump start your organization's growth engine.* New York: McGraw-Hill.

Drucker, P. (1993). *Innovation and entrepreneurship: Practice and principles.* New York: HarperBusiness.

Jaskyte, K. (2004). Transformational leadership, organizational culture, and innovativeness in nonprofit organizations. *Nonprofit Management and Leadership,* 15(2), 153–168.

Tucker, R. (2002). *Driving growth through innovation: How leading firms are transforming their futures.* San Francisco: Berrett-Koehler.

Insight #13: "We few, we happy few, we band of brothers"
The Absolute Importance of Strong, Functioning Relationships

Blake, R., & Mouton, J. (1964). *The managerial grid: The key to leadership excellence.* Houston, TX: Gulf Publishing Co.

Dansereau, F., Graen, G. G., & Haga, W. (1975). A vertical dyad linkage approach to leadership in formal organizations. *Organizational Behavior and Human Performance,* 13, 46–78.

Shakespeare, W., & Taylor, G. ed. (2008). *Henry V.* Oxford, UK: Oxford University Press.

Insight #14: Successfully Navigate Your Political Force Field
Handling the Politics of Leadership

Brandon, R., & Seldman, M. (2004). *Survival of the savvy: High-integrity political tactics for career and company success.* New York: Free Press.

Buchanan, D. A., & Badham, R. J. (2008). *Power, politics, and organizational change: Winning the turf game.* Los Angeles: SAGE.

DeLuca, J. R. (1999). *Political savvy: Systematic approaches to leadership behind-the-scenes.* Berwyn, PA: Evergreen Business Group.

McIntyre, M. G. (2005). *Secrets to winning at office politics: How to achieve your goals and increase your influence at work.* New York: St. Martin's Griffin.

Sommer, L. (2012). *Beyond office politics: The hidden story of power, affiliation & achievement in the workplace.* S.l.: Createspace.

Insight #15: Appreciate Your Friends, Allies, and Coalitions
Strengthening Your Power Base

Broom, M. (2002). *The infinite organization: Celebrating the positive use of power in organizations.* Palo Alto, CA: Davies-Black.

Hersey, P., & Goldsmith, M. (1980). A situational approach to performance planning. *Training and Development Journal,* 34(11), 38.

Kotter, J. (1985). *Power and influence.* New York: Free Press.

Vecchio, R. (2007). *Leadership: Understanding the dynamics of power and influence in organizations.* Notre Dame, IN: University of Notre Dame Press.

Insight #16: Getting What You Need
Using Your Power Base for Influence and Leverage to Get Things Done

Cialdini, R. B. (2007). *Influence: The psychology of persuasion.* New York: HarperCollins.

Cialdini, R. B. (2009). *Influence: Science and practice.* Boston: Pearson/Allyn and Bacon.

Insight #17: "To End a War"
Negotiating Your Way to Success

Fisher, R., Ury, W., & Patton, B. (2011). *Getting to yes: Negotiating agreement without giving in.* New York: Penguin.

Holbrooke, R. C. (1998). *To end a war.* New York: Random House.

Malhotra, D., & Bazerman, M. H. (2007). *Negotiation genius: How to overcome obstacles and achieve brilliant results at the bargaining table and beyond.* New York: Bantam Books.

Ury, W. (2007). *Getting past no: Negotiating in difficult situations.* New York: Bantam Books.

Insight #18: Peacetime and Wartime Decision Making
Having the Courage to Make Decisions That Count

Eisenhower, J. S. D. (2000). *Allies, Pearl Harbor to D-Day.* New York: Da Capo Press.

Nutt, P. C. (1989). *Making tough decisions: Tactics for improving managerial decision making.* San Francisco: Jossey-Bass Publishers.

Nutt, P. C. (2002). *Why decisions fail: Avoiding the blunders and traps that lead to debacles.* San Francisco: Berrett-Koehler Publishers.

Insight #19: "Life Is Tough, but It's Tougher if You're Stupid"
How to Work the Wicked Problems

Conklin, E. J. (2006). *Dialogue mapping: Building shared under-standing of wicked problems.* Chichester, UK: Wiley.

Day, G., & Schoemaker, P. (2005). Scanning the periphery. *Harvard Business Review.* Retrieved from http://hbr.harvardbusiness.org/2005/11/scanning-the-periphery/ar/1

Horn, R. E., & Weber, R. P. (2007). *New tools for resolving wicked problems: Mess mapping and resolution mapping processes.* Watertown, MA: Strategy Kinetics LLC.

Rittel, H., & Webber, M. (1973). Dilemmas in a general theory of planning. *Policy Sciences, 4,* 155–169.

Insight #20: Attack in Any Direction
How to Deal with the Pressures of Leadership

Clark, T. (2011). *Nerve: Poise under pressure, serenity under stress, and the brave new science of fear and cool.* New York: Little, Brown and Company.

Leach, J. (1994). *Survival Psychology.* Basingstoke, UK: Macmillan.

Menkes, J. (2011). *Better under pressure: How great leaders bring out the best in themselves and others.* Boston: Harvard Business Press.

Sullivan, P. (2010). *Clutch: Why some people excel under pressure and others don't.* New York: Portfolio.

Insight #21: Avoiding Tunnel Vision
Open the Aperture to Gain Perspective

Ashby, W. R. (1956). *An introduction to cybernetics.* London: Chapman & Hall.

Bertalanffy, L. (1973). *General system theory: Foundations, development, applications.* New York: G. Braziller.

Goodwin, D. K. (2005). *Team of rivals: The political genius of Abraham Lincoln.* New York: Simon & Schuster.

Gordon, L. A., & Narayanan, V. K. (1984). Management accounting systems, perceived environmental uncertainty and organization structure: An empirical investigation. *Accounting Organizations and Society,* 9(1), 33–47.

Neustadt, R. E., & May, E. R. (1988). *Thinking in time: The uses of history for decision makers.* New York: Free Press.

Rockart, J. F. (1979). Chief executives define their own data needs. *Harvard Business Review,* 30, 81–92.

Insight #22: Trusted Advisers and Mentors
The Importance of High-Quality Advice

Maister, D. H., Green, C. H., & Galford, R. M. (2001). *The trusted advisor.* New York: Touchstone.

Zachary, L. J., & Fischler, L. A. (2009). *The mentee's guide: Making mentoring work for you.* San Francisco: Jossey-Bass.

Insight #23: Losing a Battle but Not the War
Learning from Failure

Fortune, J., & Peters, G. (1995). *Systems and failures: Cases and methods.* Chichester, UK: John Wiley.

Harvard Business Review Failure Issue. (2011, April). Retrieved February 2, 2014, from http://hbr.org/archive-toc/BR1104

Insight #24: "Twelve O'Clock High"
Rebuilding Distressed Organizations

Bar-Or, Y. (2009). *Leveraging people for a corporate turnaround: Leadership and management guidance for organizational change.* Springfield, NJ: TLB Publishing.

O'Callaghan, S. (2010). *Turnaround leadership: Making decisions, rebuilding trust and delivering results after a crisis.* London: Kogan Page.

Vance, D. E. (2009). *Corporate restructuring: From cause analysis to execution.* Heidelberg, GE: Springer.

Insight #25: Communicate Like Churchill
Inspire Through Authenticity

Bolton, R. (1986). *People skills: How to assert yourself, listen to others, and resolve conflicts.* New York: Simon & Schuster.

Fairhurst, G. T. (2010). *The power of framing: Creating the language of leadership.* San Francisco: Jossey-Bass.

Fairhurst, G. T., & Sarr, R. A. (1996). *The art of framing: Managing the language of leadership.* San Francisco: Jossey-Bass Publishers.

Insight #26: "Under-the-Oak-Tree Counseling"
Build Trust with Your People

Burke, C. S, Sims, D. E., Lazzara, E. H., & Salas, E. (2007). Trust in leadership: A multi-level review and integration. *Leadership Quarterly,* 18(6), 606–632.

Covey, S. M. R., & Merrill, R. R. (2006). *The speed of trust: The one thing that changes everything.* New York: Free Press.

Dirks, K. T., & Ferrin, D. L. (2002). Trust in leadership: Meta-analytic findings and implications for organizational research. *Journal of Applied Psychology,* 87, 611–628.

Hurley, R. F. (2012). *The decision to trust: How leaders create high-trust organizations.* San Francisco: Jossey-Bass.

Lewicki, R. J., Wiethoff, C., & Tomlinson, E. C. (2005). What is the role of trust in organizational justice? *Handbook of Organizational Justice,* 247–270.

McAllister, D. J. (1995). Affect- and cognition-based trust as foundations for interpersonal cooperation in organizations. *Academy of Management Journal,* 38(1), 24–59.

Scandura, T. A., & Pellegrini, E. K. (2008). Trust and leader-member exchange (LMX): A closer look at relational vulnerability. *Journal of Leadership and Organizational Studies,* 15(2), 101–110.

Insight #27: "Dear Mrs. Ryan"
The Power of Empathetic Communication

Back, A., Arnold, R. M., & Tulsky, J. A. (2009). *Mastering communication with seriously ill patients: Balancing honesty with empathy and hope.* Cambridge, UK: Cambridge University Press.

Ioannidou, F., & Konstantikaki, V. (2008). Empathy and emotional intelligence: What is it really about? *International Journal of Caring Sciences,* 1(3), 118–123.

Lewicki, R. J., & Bunker, B. B. (1995). *Trust in relationships: A model of development and decline.* Athens, OH: Ohio State University.

Lewicki, R. J., & Bunker, B. B. (1996). Developing and maintaining trust in work relationships. In Kramer, R. M., & Tyler, T. R. (Eds.), *Trust in organizations: Frontiers of theory and reach,* 114–39. Thousand Oaks, CA: Sage Publications.

Silverman, J., Kurtz, S., & Draper, J. (2005). *Skills for communicating with patients.* Oxon, UK: Radcliffe Medical Press.

Insight #28: "Bad News Doesn't Get Better With Time"
Delivering Bad News

Ackley, D. S. (1992). *The secret of communicating bad news to employees.* IABC Communication World.

Fink, S. (2013). *Crisis communications: The definitive guide to managing the message.*

Insight #29: Commander's Intent
Empowering Your People to Adapt and Act

Shattuck, L. G. (2000). Communicating intent and imparting presence. *Military Review,* 66–72.

US Department of Defense (1992). *Conduct of the Persian Gulf War: Final Report to Congress.* Washington, DC: US Department of Defense.

US Department of Defense. (2011). Joint Publication 3-0: Joint Operations. Retrieved from Chairman of the Joint Chiefs of Staff website: http://www.dtic.mil/doctrine/new_pubs/jp3_0.pdf

Vego, M. (2010). Operational Commander's Intent (57). Retrieved from National Defense University website: http://www.ndu.edu/press/lib/images/jfq-57/vego-operationalCommanders.pdf

Insight #30: "Everything in War Is Simple, but the Simplest Thing Is Difficult"
No-Hassle Time Management

Allen, D. (2001). *Getting things done: The art of stress-free productivity.* New York: Viking.

Covey, S. R. (2000). *The 7 habits of highly effective people: Wisdom and insight from Stephen R. Covey.* Philadelphia: Running Press.

Insight #31: The Stand-Up
How to Run Great Meetings

Doyle, M., & Straus, D. (1993). *How to make meetings work!: The new interaction method.* New York: Berkeley Books.

Kirkpatrick, D. L., & American Society for Training and Development. (2006). *How to conduct productive meetings: Strategies, tips, and tools to ensure your next meeting is well planned and effective.* Alexandria, VA: ASTD Press.

Micale, F. A. (2004). *Meetings made easy: The ultimate fix-it guide.* Irvine, CA: Entrepreneur Press.

Insight #32: "Adapt, Improvise, Overcome"
Coaching Your Team

Hawkins, P. (2012). *Creating a coaching culture: Developing a coaching strategy for your organization.* Maidenhead, UK: Open University Press.

Van Nieuwerburgh, C. (2013). *An introduction to coaching skills: A practical guide.* Sage Publications Ltd.

Wilson, C. (2014). *Performance coaching: A complete guide to best practice approaches.*

Insight #33: "The Snowstorm Has Stopped"
Ask Powerful Questions

Rumsfeld, D. H. (2011). The Rumsfeld Papers. Retrieved February 2, 2014, from http://papers.rumsfeld.com/library/catalog/20052006-snowflakes

Stoltzfus, T. (2008). *Coaching questions: A coach's guide to powerful asking skills.* Virginia Beach, VA: Tony Stoltzfus.

Insight #34: Spartans at Thermopylae
Inculcating Esprit de Corps

Macey, W. H. (2009). *Employee engagement: Tools for analysis, practice, and competitive advantage.* Chichester, UK: Wiley-Blackwell.

Insight #35: Giving Your Best Military Advice
Managing Your Boss

Tulgan, B. (2010). *It's okay to manage your boss: The step-by-step program for making the best of your most important relationship at work.* San Francisco: Jossey-Bass.

Wisinski, J. (1999). Building a partnership with your boss: A take-charge assistant book. New York: AMACOM.

Insight #36: The Incredible Initiative of Airman Lateer
Leading from Below

Cohen, A. R., & Bradford, D. L. (2005). *Influence without authority.* Hoboken, NJ: Wiley.

Cohen, A. R., & Bradford, D. L. (2012). *Influencing up.* Hoboken, NJ: Wiley.

Goldsmith, M., Morgan, H. J., & Ogg, A. J. (2004). *Leading organizational learning: Harnessing the power of knowledge.* San Francisco: Jossey-Bass.

Useem, M. (2001). *Leading up: How to lead your boss so you both win.* New York: Three Rivers Press.

Insight #37: Building Future Leaders
Succession Planning

Charan, R. (2008). *Leaders at all levels: Deepening your talent pool to solve the succession crisis.* San Francisco: Jossey-Bass.

Charan, R., Drotter, S. J., & Noel, J. L. (2001). *The leadership pipeline: How to build the leadership-powered company.* San Francisco: Jossey-Bass.

Rothwell, W. J. (2010). *Effective succession planning: Ensuring leadership continuity and building talent from within.* New York: AMACOM.

Insight #38: Making Rank
Moving Up in Your Career

Asher, D. (2007). *Who gets promoted, who doesn't, and why: 10 things you'd better do if you want to get ahead.* Berkeley, CA: Ten Speed Press.

Chambers, H. (1999). *Getting promoted: Real strategies for advancing your career.* Reading, MA: Perseus Books.

Insight #39: Achieving Warrior Resilience
Develop Your Internal Reserves

Thompson, H. L. (2010). *The stress effect: Why smart leaders make dumb decisions—and what to do about it.* San Francisco: Jossey-Bass.

Insight #40: Get Your PT In
Take Care of Yourself

Thompson, H. L. (2010). *The stress effect: Why smart leaders make dumb decisions—and what to do about it.* San Francisco: Jossey-Bass.

Insight #41: Be Family Strong
Take Care of Your Family

Friedman, S. D., & Greenhaus, J. H. (2000). *Work and family—allies or enemies?: What happens when business professionals confront life choices.* Oxford, UK: Oxford University Press.

Merrill, A. R., & Merrill, R. R. (2004). *Life matters: Creating a dynamic balance of work, family, time, & money.* New York: McGraw-Hill.

Insight #42: We Appreciate You
Serve Your Community

Burke, E. M. (1999). *Corporate community relations: The principle of the neighbor of choice.* Westport, CT: Quorum Books.

Kotler, P., & Lee, N. (2005). *Corporate social responsibility: Doing the most good for your company and your cause.* Hoboken, NJ: Wiley.

Lakin, N., & Scheubel, V. (2010). *Corporate community involvement: The definitive guide to maximizing your business' societal engagement.* Stanford, CA: Stanford University Press.

Insight #43: Setting the Conditions for Your People to Perform
Your Role in Motivation

Hackman, J. R., & Oldham, G. R. (1980). *Work redesign.* Reading, MA: Addison-Wesley.

Herzberg, F., Mausner, B., & Snyderman, B. B. (1993). *The motivation to work.* New Brunswick, NJ: Transaction Publishers.

Latham, G. P. (2012). *Work motivation: History, theory, research, and practice.* Thousand Oaks, CA: SAGE.

Maslow, A. H. (1943). A theory of human motivation. *Psychological Review, 50*(4), 370.

Pinder, C. C. (2008). *Work motivation in organizational behavior.* New York: Psychology Press.

Vroom, V. H. (1982). *Work and motivation.* Malabar, FL:
R.E. Krieger Publishing Company.

Insight #44: Acknowledge Success
Celebrate Your Victories Large and Small

Weinstein, M. (1997). *Managing to have fun.* New York:
Simon & Schuster.

Insight #45: Bestowing Medals and Awards
Show Your People You Love Them

Deeprose, D. (1994). *How to recognize & reward employees.*
New York: AMACOM, American Management Association.

Insight #46: Moving Beyond Self
Cultivate Humility in Service

Collins, J. C. (2001). *Good to great: Why some companies make the
leap—and others don't.* New York: HarperBusiness.

Kraemer, H. M. J. (2011). *From values to action: The four principles
of values-based leadership.* San Francisco: Jossey-Bass.

Morris, J. A., Brotheridge, C. M., & Urbanski, J. C. (2005). Bringing
humility to leadership: Antecedents and consequences of leader
humility. *Human Relations,* 58(10), 1323–1350.

Insight #47: Working for Napoleon
How to Deal With Negative Leadership

Lubit, R. H. (2003). *Coping with toxic managers, subordinates …
and other difficult people: Using emotional intelligence to survive
and prosper.* Upper Saddle River, NJ: FT Prentice Hall.

Lubit, R. H. (2003). The tyranny of toxic managers: An emotional
intelligence approach to dealing with difficult personalities. *Ivey
Business Journal.* Retrieved from http://iveybusinessjournal.com/
topics/the-workplace/the-tyranny-of-toxic-managers-an-emotional-
intelligence-approach-to-dealing-with-difficult-personalities#.
Uw6bCYW8nag

Tate, B. W. (2011). *Bad to the bone: Empirically defining and measuring negative leadership.* S.l.: Proquest, Umi Dissertatio.

Insight #48: What to Do When the Worst Occurs
Dealing with Tragedy

Hazen, M. A. (2008). Grief and the workplace. *The Academy of Management Perspectives*, 22(3), 78–86.

Jeffreys, J. (1995). *Coping with workplace change: Dealing with loss and grief.* Mississauga, ON: Crisp Learning.

Thompson, N. (2009). *Loss, grief, and trauma in the workplace.* Amityville, NY: Baywood Publishing.

Insight #49: Commanding the Room
Leading with Presence

Scouller, J. (2011). *The three levels of leadership: How to develop your leadership presence, knowhow and skill.* Oxford, UK: Management Books 2000.

INDEX

THE LEADERSHIP CRUCIBLE
WE FORGE LEADERS

FREE 4-PART LEADERSHIP COURSE ($97 Value)
"New Leader 101"

➤ 4-part course on becoming a new leader
➤ PLUS a bonus introductory lesson
➤ AND a FREE e-book: "Essential Leadership Concepts"

Here's what you'll learn:

Lesson 1: Why Do You Want to Be a Leader?
• Explore what it means to be a leader
• Discover your motivation to lead

Lesson 2: What's Your Definition of Leadership?
• Build your own definition of leadership

Lesson 3: What's Your Leadership Philosophy?
• See examples that might work for you
• Develop your own leadership philosophy

Lesson 4: What to Do Your First Day on the Job
• Step-by-step process to start off on the right foot
• What your people want to know about you
• How to make your first meeting a success

**Follow the link below to access your
FREE LEADERSHIP MINI-COURSE!**

www.theleadershipcrucible.com/new-leader-101-access

Or scan this QR code: